Advanced Praise for

Greatness Awaits You! is not another celebration of words but is one that is compelling and courageous in an attempt to create hope to encourage all mankind.

Mr. Clive Brown
Cape Town, South Africa

Carlos and I have been friends over 20 years! My how time flies. Over the years he has become a man of faith, a great family man, a dynamic speaker, and a gifted writer as you will see in *Greatness Awaits You*!

Keith Davis
Pittsburgh, PA

To Vincent

You are creator to greatness!

GREATNESS Awaits You!

Best,
Cordo T Cook

Greatness Awaits You! 23 Ways to Unlock the Greatness Within!
Copyright © 2021 by Carlos T. Carter and Seeds2Fruit Motivation ®

ISBN: 978-1-7379281-0-2

Published by: Seeds2fruit Motivation ®
Printed in the United States of America

Author Photos: Emmai Aliquiva & Ya Momz House, Inc.
Internal Layout and Design: InSCRIBEd Inspiration, LLC.
Edited by: Carlos T. Carter, Mila Sanina, Penda L. James, Angelica Perry, Janese Dillingham, Krystle Morrison & Kaitlyn Nykwest
Cover Design: Hossam G.
Photo p. 75 used in meme: Ahmad Sandidge

All real-life anecdotes are told with permission from actual parties involved and recorded to the best of the author's recollection. Names in some instances have not been used at the request of the individuals referenced. In some cases, parties mentioned are deceased. Details of some instances have been slightly modified to enhance readability, or to ensure privacy. Any resemblance of any other parties is purely coincidental.

All rights reserved. No part of this book may be reproduced or transmitted in any form electronic, or mechanical, including photocopying and recording, or held in any information storage and retrieval system without permission in writing from the author and publisher.

All scriptures from THE HOLY BIBLE, NEW INTERNATIONAL VERSION®, NIV® Copyright © 1973, 1978, 1984, 2011 by Biblica, Inc.™ Used by permission. All rights reserved worldwide.

All direct quotations from Holy Scripture are from the King James Version (KJV) and are in the public domain in the United States of America. For the United Kingdom, said extracts from the Authorized Version of the Bible (The King James Bible), the rights in which are vested in the Crown, are reproduced by permission of the Crown's Patentee, Cambridge University Press.

GREATNESS Awaits You!

The Beginning 1
The Middle 11
The Now 25

23 WAYS TO UNLOCK THE GREATNESS WITHIN 33

1 - About Those Thoughts 35
2 - What Does It Take To Succeed? 41
3 - 11 Keys To Leadership 51
4 - Faith Matters! 63
5 - The Power Of Yes & No 69
6 - Healthy & Holistic Living 77
7 - Lead With Passion & Purpose 85
8 - Don't Settle 93
9 - Take Risks 99
10 - Live To Give! 107
11 - The Pursuit Of Excellence 115
12 - Vote For You! 125
13 - Different Is Dope! 133
14 - Believe In Change 139
15 - No Shortcuts, Please! 147
16 - Get Out Of Your Comfort Zone 155

17 - Don't Sweat It 163
18 - Face Your Fears 173
19 - Stay Connected 185
20 - Believe In Yourself 199
21 - Understand Your Value And Fit 211
22 - Keep It Real 221
23 - Who You Are When No One Is Looking ... 229

GET ON THE ROAD TO GREATNESS 236

ACKNOWLEDGEMENTS

- **Marcia my soulmate** — We were created for each other! Your love fuels my soul! Thanks for helping me be a better man and person.
- **Elijah, Daylon, and Isaiah** — Anything is possible for you when you live your passion and purpose! You are my pride and joy!
- **My grandmother, Pearl** — Thanks for loving and accepting me unconditionally.
- **My mother** — Thanks for your sacrifices and reminding me that I can do anything.
- **My father, Nehemiah**—Thanks for coming into my life when I needed you most. You gave me the fatherly love that I desperately longed for. RWG!
- **Michael Anderson**—Thanks for believing in and supporting my vision for Seeds2fruit Motivation ® by spreading my messages of value, passion, and purpose.
- **Mila Sanina**—Thanks for believing in my book and helping me to shape my message clearly.
- **Dr. Toliver**—Thank you for pushing me towards excellence.
- **Cassandra Brentley**— For seeing my ability to inspire others and pushing me to share my inspiration.
- **Emmai Aliquiva (Ya Momz House, Inc.)** — Thanks brother for the amazing pics. You truly captured my spirit and life's journey in each pic. I guess that's what happens when you team with a 4X Emmy Award winning photographer and filmmaker. I am privileged! I have nothing but love for you!

- **Angelica Perry** – Thank you for your excellence.
- **Kaitlyn Nykwest** - Thanks for agreeing to read and check for errors. I appreciate you!
- **Penda L. James (InSCRIBEd Inspiration, LLC.)** —You are such a joy to work with. I could not ask for a better scribe coach to layout and perfect my book. You are amazing!
- Special thanks for the **B.F. Jones Memorial Library** in Aliquippa, PA for allowing us to shoot our cover photo. Your hospitality was memorable.
- **People who have been undervalued, unnoticed, and marginalized by others**—You matter. Others may doubt you, but you can unlock the greatness that is within!

FOREWORD

In so many ways, Carlos T. Carter embodies and personifies the content of his book. He invites his readers to look in, look up, look out, and look ahead. He wishes they would reflectively look inside to recognize the inherent beauty within, humbly and dependently look up and express gratitude for the grace received, generously and warmly look out for the interests of others, and with joy, hope, and courage look ahead toward a future filled with promise.

Mr. Carter, with candor and humility, opens windows into his own journey which, like most journeys, includes sunshine, detours, delays, derailments, discouragement, as well as delight and deliverance. He is an open book. He shares with vulnerability his own pain and joy, but he does this not in a self-congratulatory way, but in order to give readers the strength to face their own histories and struggles and be freed from needless guilt or shame.

Carlos knows that there is more to each person than meets the eye. He understands that, if and when individuals are reduced to a type or a brand, their dignity is diminished, and their potential is caged. But, when they see and are seen, hear and are heard, love and are loved, serve, and are served, there are boundless possibilities for goodness to flourish and prosperity to flow, both for individuals as well as communities.

I am proud of Carlos and glad to know him as a friend. I am thankful that his readers will benefit from his written guidance as I have benefited from sharing time, space, tea, and tabbouleh together with him. Together, the greatness in each multiplies and transforms.

Saleem Ghubril

PRELUDE

Growing up, I was not the best writer, but I had no trouble communicating my thoughts verbally. I wrote and submitted a copyright for a collection of poetry in my early twenties entitled, "Voices from the Soul." Poetry was therapy for me, I used to share my poems and other people seemed to enjoy them. I have not published it yet, but I may consider doing so in the future.

I am in my forties now and have not been inspired to write poetry for decades. I never in a million years would have thought that I would write a book. I started writing a blog in November 2017 as an experiment. I was nervous and had no clue how people would respond to my vulnerability. It is not easy being vulnerable, but I knew I needed to share something authentic so people could discover their greatness by learning from my challenges and triumphs.

> "...I had no clue how people would respond to my vulnerability."

Once I started writing my blog, I was blown away by people around the world reacting and connecting to my stories and messages. I was shocked to go viral two months in a row on

LinkedIn when I wrote: "Get Out: No Job is Worth Your Sanity" and "Will the Real Leaders Stand Up." My inbox blew up with emails from America to Europe and from Africa to Australia! It was humbling and inspiring since I told myself when I started, "*I don't want to be perceived as a Black writer or speaker, I want to impact people from all cultures and nations.*"

People would ask me when I'd write a book or would tell me that I needed to write a book. The constant prodding fueled my internal passion and calling to author this book. My hope is that as you read, you will be inspired and empowered to discover and live your passion and fully realize your potential. My goal is to share principles that have helped me and continue to shape my life. I do not profess to know everything or to have all the answers, but I would like to share what I know to help you become the best version of yourself.

The first section provides context to my journey with background about me. In the second section, I share 23 principles that I believe will lead you to greatness. After each section take a moment to pause, process, reflect and apply the lessons to your life. I recommend that you take your time to work through each chapter rather than reading every chapter in one sitting. I consider each chapter a daily devotional. Take a reflective approach that works best for you.

Greatness Awaits You! is for anyone in the process of finding their passion and purpose who needs a little inspiration along the way. I reference my faith and spirituality in this book, because I am a spiritual person, and my faith is part of who I am. Even if you do not believe in a higher power, I hope that you will be inspired. Even if you are successful, you may be looking to take things to the next level.

Wherever you are in your journey, greatness awaits you!

Carlos

THE BEGINNING
Childhood Memories

It was a beautiful summer day in Pittsburgh, a day of anticipation and expectation. The way I remember it, neither the clouds nor smog were hiding the sun. I was probably about seven or eight years old. My mom, my siblings and I were on the Port Authority bus going between the two mill towns on the Monongahela River connected by steel bridges: Duquesne to McKeesport. I don't remember the purpose of the trip. Most likely, we were going to Cox's, one of our favorite department stores back in the seventies. All I remember is my excitement.

As I sat in the front of the bus with my beautiful mother, I remember admiring her deep dimples and smooth ebony skin. Her smile could eclipse the darkest cloud; her looks belying her struggles as a young single mother trying to raise three children. At some point, a man sitting near us piqued my curiosity. I don't remember anything special about him, but I could see my image of a young Black boy reflected in him. I asked myself, *"Is he the one? Is he my father?"* Although I was a curious and inquisitive kid, somehow, I knew not to give voice to this question and longing.

I had never seen my father but tried to visualize what he would look like. My mom did not talk much about him but would say, "He is tall and slim, and you are built just like him." She would also say, "He used to be friends with your uncle Robert." I always hoped that my uncle would contact him and introduce us. As I stared at the man on the bus, I wondered, "Is he the one who will come claim me, his son?" But that did not happen. I do not think the man ever noticed me. This quiet search for my father, his love, and his connection was a secret longing that would one day bubble up and come to a head.

I lived in the Monongahela Valley until I was eleven. It was a time in Pittsburgh where I can remember lines of people leaving the mills at the end of their shift. A time when good paying jobs allowed the blue-collar workers to put food on the table and the working class to have a slice of the American pie. When my family moved, we relocated to the East End of Pittsburgh.

Although I was excited about this transition and living closer to my cousins, I was afraid, as any teenager would be, that I would not be able to fit in or make friends in the new neighborhood. When we first moved to the East End, we lived with my Aunt Beverly who was loving, hilarious and feisty. I do not think there was much she ever held back. When she thought about something, she had no problem talking about it. I could sit and listen to her for hours.

What I liked most about her was that she always accepted me for who I was. She was a generous, warm soul who always showed hospitality to others. Some of my fondest memories are of the times I spent with my family at Aunt Beverly's house. One especially hot summer night, my cousins, siblings, and I all slept on the front porch of her house to escape the heat inside. We had a blast laughing and joking with one another under the stars. It was great being with my family! We would have fights and disagreements, but we always reconciled, because we are family!

After staying with Aunt Bev for a month, we moved into our own house. It was the first time I recall living in a house. This was a big deal for me and my two siblings, especially after living in the Cochrandale Projects from the mid-seventies to the early eighties. I have come a long way!

My fondest childhood memories include the times I spent playing outside with my friends. I loved riding my bike, building fires to roast potatoes, catching snakes, bees, and grasshoppers, making slingshots, exploring the woods, and visiting my family. Those were the times when kids were young, wild, and free. We did not have much growing up and we learned to appreciate the small things. I especially remember the joy I felt when my friends and I got new pairs of sneakers. It was a big deal back then. Today it is a little different with my kids -- they have multiple pairs of shoes. Having very little taught me to be grateful. When I get into a complaining mode, I remind myself to count my many blessings.

During my childhood, I had many hopes and dreams. I wanted to be an actor, doctor, basketball player, firefighter, veterinarian and who knows what else. I was always dreaming of something that I could be, and my mother encouraged me by saying, "You can do anything if you put your mind to it." She also told me often, "Black is beautiful." This affirmation was important for a kid like me, growing up in the seventies and eighties when diverse role models in leadership positions was still rare.

Being dark-skinned with full lips was not always a plus. I remember people saying things like, "You are pretty for someone who is dark-skinned." It is sad that qualifier was needed, a marker of residual self-hatred and internalized racism left over from 250 years of slavery and

100 years of Jim Crow. Of course, I did not understand that it was simply internalized racism back then. This is a paradigm that devalues Blackness or anything Black and espouses the European or dominant culture's standard of beauty and value.

Even though I struggled with my complexion at times, I am thankful that my mom affirmed that Black is beautiful. Looking back, it really underscores the importance of children having healthy self-esteem and understanding their value and worth, even when their peers do not. On a positive note, when I hit eighteen, Michael Jordan was in his prime and his popularity made chocolate the "it" thing. That trend buoyed my appeal with the ladies. The rest is history!

Freedom from Trauma & Shame

During my childhood, I held a secret that would torment me for years. It filled me with pain that I tried to hide and suppress until I finally had to tell my truth! I am a survivor of sexual abuse; this experience shapes me in many ways. Although it happened when I was younger, I did not get the courage to speak about the abuse until I was nineteen years old. I remember

".. find the strength and support to move toward healing..."

watching an episode of the Oprah Winfrey Show featuring male survivors of sexual abuse. Hearing these men tell their stories encouraged me to go to a counselor. Besides my efforts to find my father, telling someone about what happened to me was one of the most courageous steps that I had ever taken.

Burdened with shame and fear, I pushed myself to reach out. My shame was based on what others might think about what I experienced and what they would think of me. When a person experiences child sexual abuse, they experience things that children should never have to deal with or be exposed to. If you are a trauma survivor, you must find the strength and support to move toward healing. Going to counseling was my path. Your trauma is not your responsibility, but you are responsible for your healing.

After finding the courage to go to counseling, one of my goals was to tell my girlfriend (now wife). After I told her about my trauma, she was loving and supportive, which was not surprising. She has been compassionate and nurturing from the day I met her. That was one of the things that drew me to her, and she has not changed! Unfortunately, I did not have the courage to tell my family until my early thirties.

Dealing with and confronting this truth was one of the most important decisions of my life. The decision to address my turmoil put me in a position to come out of the fear and shame and get on the road to pursuing my passion and purpose and living my best life. The journey has not been easy, but that courage released me from the bondage of the past and gave me the freedom to rebuild myself from the inside out.

People comment about how happy, full of life, and free I am. I have been set free. I have learned to accept myself for who I am, flaws and all, and not worry about what others think of me. Someone once said, "When you know yourself, you are empowered. When you accept yourself, you are invincible!"

A colleague from my banking days commented to me, "It takes a lot of guts to do the motivational videos and other things you do." I was surprised when he said that, but I took the time to reflect, and I realized that he is right. I was afraid when I initially set out to do my videos, but I told myself, *"I cannot let fear stop me."* I have learned that when there is a calling to do something, you must push past your fears and go after what is important to you. People tell me how my messages help them get through their day or have a better perspective and appreciation for themselves. This feedback reminds me to continue doing what God has created me to do and shows me that I am making an impact. I don't do it for money. I do it because I am passionate about leaving people and places better than I found them!

"Impossible is just a word thrown around by small men who find it easier to live in the world they've been given than to explore the power they have to change it. Impossible is not a fact. It's an opinion. Impossible is potential. Impossible is temporary. Impossible is nothing."

~Muhammad Ali

THE MIDDLE
High School Years

We often forget the challenges teenagers face. As they work to discover who they are and find out where they fit, they can struggle. High school was not easy for me. My challenges were less academic, although academically, I did not always work up to my potential. I was trying to fit in even though I had some friends. I kept to myself because I was processing the shame and challenges from the abuse. Despite this, I made it through by the grace of God.

I wasn't committed to competing in organized sports, but I briefly ran cross country and track. I really wanted to play football, but I did not have the confidence to go out for the team. I was in good shape, and the football coach would see me showing off doing pull ups in the gym. He asked me to try out for the team, but I never followed up. Ironically, my three boys excel at sports, but I never push them to play. I only ask that they complete what they start, something I did not do.

One thing I was good at in high school was singing. My first time on stage was at a talent show in tenth or eleventh grade. I was terrified, because my peers could be brutal, but they were supportive of my singing. I decided to sing

"Always and Forever" by Heatwave. I gathered the twins Don and Gary Gibbs and we put it together. We had to sing over the original song because we did not have the instrumental track. People could not believe we were singing so well.

Although my family did not really think I could sing, I always knew that I could. I really blossomed in our high school choir and was given several solos. The first was "The Christmas Song!" and then the Temptations' version of "Silent Night!" with a great singer and classmate, Lachelle Garner. She had a great talent that shown through, even though, she was shy. We sang solos at graduation. I sang John Lennon's "Imagine," and she sang "Sunrise."

One of my favorite teachers was my English teacher Dr. Brenda Toliver. Our relationship did not start off on the right foot, but she helped influence my positive high school trajectory. She went from one of my worst teachers to one of my best. After her class, I improved from high average grades to high honor roll. When I started her class in eleventh grade, we had a conflict. A fellow student challenged me to say, "Sunshine City" quickly several times, which resulted in "City" turning into a curse word. When Dr. Toliver heard it, she was furious. She told me that she wanted me to write 100 times, "I will not use my mouth as a waste receptacle."

Feisty and rebellious, I refused to do the writing assignment. I was a stubborn soul - I talked to the principal to contest. I went as far as contacting the administration's office. Dr. Toliver would not allow me to return to class until I completed the assignment. I ended up wandering around school like a ship without a sail. After a few weeks, I caved in and completed the assignment.

Dr. Toliver was known as the hardest teacher in the school, but I received many A's in her class. Students loved her because she challenged us, really cared for us, and was open about sharing her life's mistakes and triumphs with us. She encouraged us not to settle for less. Whenever we used language that was not proper, she would put it on the board, and we all got a kick out of it. Dr. Toliver encouraged us to set goals, walk and talk with authority and confidence, and be proud of who we were. She was the first teacher to speak with such candor to me, and I loved it and embraced it.

In addition to reading Shakespeare and other writers, we read *The Autobiography of Malcolm X*, *Native Son* by Richard Wright, and *Man-child in the Promise Land* by Claude Brown. Students, Black and white, could not put these books down or stop talking about what we were reading. I had never seen anything like this before in school. The books exposed me to more of my culture, otherwise absent from the public school system, and gave me a greater sense of pride and connection I had never had.

I credit Dr. Toliver's class for developing my vocabulary and public speaking skills. I learned and memorized over four hundred words and recited my first speech. I was a class clown and seemed to have the knack for making everyone laugh hysterically without even trying. I recall my opening line: "Good morning, class! I would like to introduce you to a very important person, myself, Carlos Carter!" I did not lack gall! I told them about my career aspirations and about an embarrassing moment in preschool when I thought I was a superhero and knocked the kids off the monkey bars. I told the teachers that my mother would not do anything about it. Boy, was I wrong! My mother gave me a deserved whooping and I have been good ever since. I credit Dr. Toliver for loving her students and pushing us towards excellence. She taught us to never settle for less than our best.

Honoring Dr. Toliver

In August 2018, I was honored to deliver one of my most important motivational speeches at Woodland Hills School District near Pittsburgh. This was not my alma mater, nor the school where Dr. Toliver taught. The district was looking to encourage four hundred and fifty educators before kicking off the 2018-19 school year. This district had lost several students in the district, including Antwon Rose, Jr., who was killed by a police officer. His murder sparked protests by students and the greater Pittsburgh community.

Before the presentation, one of the administrators mentioned that they might be a tough crowd. I told her, "I guarantee that I can touch their hearts and remind them of not what they do, but why they do it." I entitled my speech, "How My Teacher Changed My Life!" I received a standing ovation, and many people were in tears! I can't completely take credit for the great response.

No one knew that Dr. Toliver was in the audience. She thought she was coming to hear me speak, but to her surprise, I honored her with the "Best Teacher and Mentor Ever" award and it moved to tears. She accepted the award and flowers and I handed her the microphone, and she expressed the importance of loving her students like her family! The audience was moved by her words! Ironically, when I picked her up, she said, "God told me that one day I will know what impact I had on my students!" She had no clue how quickly her premonition would come to fruition.

Left Photo	My high school yearbook photo
Right Photo	Me with Dr. Toliver

College Student and a Young Father

During my senior year of high school, I was determined to go to college. I knew that college was my ticket to a better life. At first I wanted to become a lawyer, but I did not pursue that route. For some reason I was under the impression that lawyers had to lie, and I was not comfortable with that. I chose General Studies at the community college where I received an associate's degree.

I met Marcia, my beautiful wife of twenty six years, in March 1990 on Community College of Allegheny County campus. My cousins from Gary, Indiana, introduced us during my first semester and we became inseparable instantly. We had a lot in common and she was a sweet girl. By our second semester, within eleven months of our first date, she found out she was pregnant. This was challenging for both of us, but especially me. I was ambitious and had dreams of going to Howard University for Law. I wanted to go overseas to Spain or Latin America as an exchange student.

I was immature and did not know how to be a father, especially since I did not have many examples around me growing up. Although things were shaky at times, we figured it out together and raised a great son named Elijah! I knew that I would not abandon my son the way my father had abandoned me. I was going make sure that I would be there for my son and provide for my family.

Shortly after Elijah's birth, I graduated from community college and transferred to the University of Pittsburgh, where I earned a Bachelor of Business Administration. I then went to Robert Morris University and earned my MBA with a concentration in finance. Thanks to encountering Dr. Toliver, I continued to excel in school, and I graduated with honors.

After getting my Bachelor's Degree, I was working at a local hospital when my mentor saw something in me. One day he said, "I like you! You would interview well. Give me your resumé, and I will share it with my wife who is head of corporate staffing." He helped me get an interview at Mellon Bank, National Association (MBNA). That was a blessing of anticipation and expectation that continues to guide my life.

Becoming a Banker

I worked in banking for eighteen years. I worked my way up from operations to credit analysis, I was a relationship manager and eventually was promoted to become a Senior Vice President. This evolution was not easy. There were not many people who looked like me in the corporate world. I had to learn to become comfortable with being uncomfortable.

Although there were good times, there were challenges I had to navigate, including a dominant culture where I did not always fit in. I had to endure microaggressions (insulting comments) and environments that were racially insensitive. I worked with people who were very privileged, but I resolved to stay positive. I had my cheerful outlook, boldness, kindness, and work ethic going for me. People usually liked me and that is good. However, I am sure there were people who did not like me, and that is OK. I was not there to win a popularity contest. Working in banking was good for me financially but it was not fulfilling. I felt boxed in and not able to use all of my talents. Not to mention the product pushing I had to oversee, which focused on making sales rather than meaningful client solutions. Still, I liked the challenge of sales, being innovative, and making an impact in the community. I really enjoyed coaching business owners and helping them fulfill their dreams.

About My Father, Nehemiah Antonio Brazil

You may be wondering about my father. I am glad to say that we did end up meeting when I was twenty-four years old. I was married a month before we met. It is funny how the very thing you could be looking for is right in front of you. One day, I was talking to my brother Ronique about wanting to find my father and he said, "I know where he is!"

"What?!"

"My friend Steve lives on the Northside, and he knows who he is!" Just like that, my brother contacted his friend and gave me an address. Ironically, he lived down the street from my high school. Sometimes a friend of mine would fix my car in the alley behind his house and I had no clue my father lived there! I would ride by his street during high school and had no clue that he lived so close by!

I did not know if my father was interested in meeting me. I was fearful of his rejection and had lots of crazy thoughts. Despite my fears, I got the courage to write him a letter. I never realized before then that I had internalized anger about him. As I wrote the letter, I felt it bubble up for the first time. I told him that I wanted to meet him and that he did not have to tell his family about me. I told him I wanted to know why he chose to turn his back on me. I also said, "Despite everything, that I love you. It was time for Black fathers to step up and break the cycle of fatherlessness.

I found the courage to mail the letter and included a picture of me with my wife and son. It was one of the most difficult things I had done up to that point. The address was incorrect, but it was only off by two doors. His neighbor took it to him. My father read the letter and called me. The message on my answering machine said something like, "This is your dad. I have been looking for you all these years and I want to meet you and tell my family about you." He told me in our first phone conversation that my letter moved him to tears. It took a while, but I warmed up to him.

Our first meeting was awkward, and I felt numb. We went to dinner with my stepmother, wife and son Elijah who was about three. To the right is a picture of the day we met. My father was easygoing, and we talked on the phone all the time. He would invite me over for meals and eventually, I became comfortable enough to

21

call him "Dad." He had other kids that he was not close to, but as he began building a relationship with me, he and his other children also grew closer.

I loved giving my dad gifts on Christmas. He would quietly accept them, and I would learn later that it meant the world to him. He would later say that he always wondered why his life was empty but realized it was because he wasn't close to his children.

As time passed, I became close to my father and his family. After he died on July 31, 2006, following a yearlong long battle with lung cancer, I became president of the family reunion. What irony, going from not being known by the family for 24 years to becoming the reunion president! My father died on my eleventh wedding anniversary. The good news is that I was able to be there for him. He is gone but never forgotten.

Although my dad was macho, he had no problem telling me how much he loved me. He was proud of me, and I would become embarrassed when he bragged about me to others, until I realized that it was his way of showing love. I am thankful that I received the love and affirmation of my father. We had eleven years together, but, as they say it is not about how many years, but how many miles. We put in a lot of miles together, and I thank God for the courage to find him and ultimately find myself in the process. Getting to know my father helped complete me as a man and set me up for greater success. More importantly, it helped me help other men who are also fatherless.

Photo | Photo with My Dad at my first concert at a local church in Mt. Olive Church in Rankin, PA. He was so proud!

THE NOW
The Transformation of a Banker: Living My Passion and Purpose

I left my career in banking because I wanted to do something more fulfilling. I wanted to be in a better position to leverage my leadership skills and passion to benefit the community. That opportunity came when I was employed in a role that was not working out, and I was let go. The company was going to let me try to relocate, but I did not want to move during my son's junior year of high school.

Around that time, I was offered a job at a local nonprofit, but I made my case to be a consultant for the company; I was not sure that I wanted to take on a full time job at that point. In this role, I helped start a school and was working to create an admissions department. I had never done anything like this before, but I understood business and business development. Our team figured it out. It was a challenging and humbling experience that made me better.

I tried going into another banking role for about six months. It was a disaster and not a good fit. I became depressed and felt like a complete failure. After months of self-reflection, discovery, and rebuilding, I had a better sense of my purpose and passion, which allowed me to emerge with greater focus. It was not a painless process, but a critical journey for me. With prayer and support from friends, family, and a counselor, I was able to get back on my feet. This experience taught me to appreciate my value apart from my job. It grew me more than any other experience and humbled and positioned me to empower and motivate others.

Although it was a tough experience, I am stronger, wiser, more focused, and better positioned to make an impact in the world. After the last stint in banking, I returned to consult with the same nonprofit for another year.

I am living my passion as a nonprofit leader. I have worked in banking, in the medical field, and within the educational system. With Homeless Children's Education Fund (HCEF) I worked to create educational opportunities to help young people break the cycle of poverty. Currently, I empower African Americans and other marginalized communities to achieve economic self-reliance, parity, power, and civil rights. I also live my passion by giving motivational speeches and seminars to empower others to become better people and leaders.

Top Left	Me with Colin Powell. He was retired from being the first-African American Secretary of State. I met him while receiving the 2013 National Diversity Leadership Award at California University of PA (2013)
Top Right	Me giving my Different is Dope inspirational talk at North Allegheny School District with my kindergarten pic in the background. Was for their "Celebration of Us" diversity event (2019)
Bottom Left	Speaking at Woodland Hills High School "How My Teacher Changed My Life!" (2018)
Bottom Right	Pic at the Children's Museum of Pittsburgh accepting the "Ted Craig Humanitarian of the Year Award" from Women's Center & Shelter of Greater Pittsburgh for our work at HCEF (2018)

Top Left	My favorite vacation photo in Wildwood, NJ (2019)
Top Right	Pic with my mom at a Christmas Party (2015)
Bottom Left	Family Photo with my wife and sons Daylon, Isaiah, Elijah at Myrtle Beach South Carolina (2021)
Bottom Right	The sunset behind Marcia and I attending a wedding in California at Loews Coronado Bay Resort (2021)

Family photo with my mom and siblings at my mom's retirement party (2019)

Top Left	Pic with my brother Nehemiah Brazil (2021)
Top Left	Pic with my good friend Jason J. Washington at my 40th Birthday Celebration
Bottom Left	Pic at the Pittsburgh Jazz Festival with one of our favorite couple friends David and DeVona Hopkins
Bottom Right	Race pic with my friend David at the EQT 10 Miler Race

Top Left	Early 90s Young Love pic with my girlfriend and now wife Marcia
Left Middle	Wedding Day in front of church before going to the reception (July 1995)
Bottom Left	Throwback pic with my dear mother in-law. She loved me like her own...RWG!
Right	Pic of my beloved Maternal grandmother, Pearl

"If you expect failure, you will get failure, but if you expect to succeed, I am sure you will succeed."

~Dr. Norman Vincent Peal
(The Power of Positive Thinking, p. 94)

23 WAYS TO UNLOCK THE GREATNESS WITHIN

1 – ABOUT THOSE THOUGHTS
Your Thoughts Will Make or Break You

I often run into people who believe the world is not going in the right direction, and that we live in divisive times. Although I cannot argue that there are many challenges and concerns in the world, I must believe that good people outnumber bad people; it is a matter of focus. If we focus on the negative or expect the negative, we will find it.

Before I get out of bed in the morning, the first thing I do is grab my phone to turn off the alarm. I read my daily devotional, meditate, and pray to put myself in the right mind frame before I start my day. In my pursuit of positivity, I am often distracted by news alerts or updates related to the negative political environment. Most times, I avoid distractions, but there are times when I succumb!

Many years ago, my family purchased a minivan. Prior to that date, I did not realize how many minivans were around. After our purchase, I paid more attention to them since I had one.

The Power of Positive Thinking by Dr. Norman Vincent Peal encourages people to be more conscientious about the power of thoughts and more careful about the thoughts that flow in and out of their minds. This is important because our thoughts can make us or break us! He says,

"If you expect the best, you are given some strange kind of power to create the conditions that produce the desired results (p. 98)." Although most understand on the surface that our thinking can affect us negatively or positively, we don't always grasp the true depth and impact our thoughts have on our mind, body, spirit, and quality of life. Further, our thoughts impact our ability to live and lead with passion and purpose!

I remember a conversation I had with a man who shared that he continued to face many challenges. The root of his challenges were in the toxic words of his father telling him he would never amount to anything. Although his father is deceased, this man continues to be haunted by these words and thoughts. They drowned out the promise of his potential. I encouraged him to unlearn the lies and words of his father and replace them with words of power and affirmation.

Although you may not have a situation as extreme as this man, you can think of times when you have thought negative thoughts about yourself that have put limitations on your ability to start a business, go for a promotion or live your best life. A few years ago, as I transitioned into a new leadership role, I had to deal with some challenging and pessimistic personalities. I stayed positive by telling myself, *"These challenges will grow me as a person and leader and position me for greater opportunities."* I am proud to say that, despite many bumps and bruises along the way, these thoughts have come to fruition. I could have easily fallen into moping and despair, but instead made the decision to entertain positive rather than negative thoughts. I did have some periods of negativity and deep frustration, but in the end, I resolved to move in a more positive direction.

Starting today, watch your thought life! Think thoughts that will edify you and others. Corral and release negative thoughts and immediately replace them with positivity. Guard your thoughts daily knowing that they have the power to change your life for better or worse! Change your thoughts, and you will change your life!

What can you do to have more positive thoughts? Well, I am glad you asked! Feed your mind what you want to grow, count your blessings daily, let your light shine, and turn on your light for others to see.

- Only Feed What You Want to Grow - Thoughts and intentions are like plants and seeds. Have you ever had a plant that could survive weeks without watering and proper care? What happened? It probably died!

Similarly, if you want to be more positive, stop feeding your mind negativity! Just like the plant, negativity will die if you stop feeding it. Turn off the news and walk away from or redirect negative conversations. Feed your mind more positivity, and positivity will abound! There is a battle of two wolves in our minds, one is positive, and one is negative. The one you feed is the one that wins.

- Count Your Blessings Daily – Sometimes people spend so much time adding up their troubles that they forget to count their blessings. Every day, try to find three things that you are thankful for and meditate on them. I guarantee you it will make you feel more positive! Living life with joy is a choice you make when you take time to count your blessings. Be grateful!

- Let Your Light Shine - Don't succumb to the temptation of negativity. Always focus on the best in yourself and others. Make a point to give sincere compliments to those around you. By seeing, exhorting, and honoring the best in others, you let your light shine and that will be a gateway for others to do the same! This approach will create more positivity for everyone!

- Turn on Your Light - I don't want people to think that I am a positive person 100 percent of the time, or that I never succumb to negativity. I make the conscious decision to count my blessings daily and try to look for good in every situation.

- Finally, find a reason to smile and make others smile. Make a deliberate effort to focus on and feed the positive no matter what! This mindset shift will create more positive energy in the universe. Turn on your light and let it shine for others to see!

FOR REFLECTION
"If we focus on the negative or expect the negative, we will find it."
~Carlos T. Carter

- Write down some negative thoughts that are visiting your mind.
- For each thought, write down a positive affirmation you can use to counter the negative thoughts.
- Make a list of things or people who bring negativity into your life and create daily rituals or strategies to help you counter or challenge them.

2 – WHAT DOES IT TAKE TO SUCCEED?
The Formula for Success

Each of us is wired and shaped differently; some are structured thinker/planner types while others are free spirited. There are pros and cons to each approach: free-spirited people are more creative and spontaneous, and they probably have more fun. On the other hand, they are sometimes not as focused and can then find themselves stressed at the last minute trying to meet deadlines. Structured people who are more deliberate plan everything and probably do not tap into their creative side as often as they should. They can be perceived as too uptight.

My wife and I reflect these differences. Although I can be spontaneous, I am mostly a structured thinker/planner. My spontaneity comes into play when I pop up and say: "Let's go here" or "Let's do this" or "I am going to go for a run or go to karaoke" - it can just come from nowhere.

I am spontaneous for inspirational videos and messages. My dominant thinker/planner personality is often demonstrated before each day or start of the week, because I write down the important things I want to accomplish. My wife, on the other hand, would almost never do that. She knows that there are things she needs to do but will do them as she thinks of it. Then, at the last minute she will run around trying to get things accomplished. I admire her ability to live in the moment!

Despite different personality types or inclinations to be one way or the other, you can benefit from goal setting! If you do not set goals, you are aiming nowhere and will hit something random every time. Is it what you want to hit? Live intentionally.

Anybody who has lived long enough understands that life has twists and turns, and it is not difficult to wake up one day and wonder how you got to a certain point, or why you did not accomplish something that you wanted to accomplish.

Some say there is no formula for success, and they are partly right. There are things you can do to create success in your life. Here is my formula for success:

Goal + Plan + Focus + Determination = Success

Setting Goals

A goal is something that you want to accomplish. This book only exists because I set a goal and put in work. You cannot base your goals on where you are now. Rather, they should be based on where you want to be. Create goals that challenge you!

When I was around six or eight, I used to tell my mother that I wanted to be the president of the United States. It didn't occur to me at the time no U.S. presidents looked like me; that was good; otherwise, I may have limited what was possible for me (By the way, I forgot about that goal as I got older, but I'm glad Barack Obama stepped in for me).

Have an element of dreaming in your goals and have the capacity to see beyond where you are today. Use that goal of what could be as your motivation to move forward and achieve whatever you want in life. It is never okay to not set any goals. Everyone should aspire to do something; we all have God-given talents that were not meant to sit on the shelf. If we don't set goals, then what do we have to aspire towards? Do you want to roam around aimlessly and end up with regrets?

I want to encourage you to be realistic in setting your goals. At the same time, you need to have bold dreams that challenge you. Many things we now take for granted started as bold dreams. Neil Armstrong touched down on the moon in 1969 with six hundred million people watching in amazement on grainy television screens. He said, "That's one small step for man, one giant leap for mankind," and became the manifestation of a collective American dream.

This dream was the manifestation of a promise by John F. Kennedy years earlier to land a man on the moon. Be realistic, but do not limit the possibilities! No matter what, keep an element of faith in your dreams, see it through. We talk more about faith in principle four.

So, What's The Plan?

This is a question that I utter often to my wife when she wants to do something. If you have a goal or dream, you must create a plan. Even this book that you are reading was created with a plan. I had wanted to write a book for a while, but I did not have a plan. I had to eventually come up with one, otherwise, you would not be reading, and I would not have been able to accomplish my goal.

Planning is creating a roadmap. Back in the day people would have used a map or visited AAA to get a TripTik (paper equivalent of GPS Direction) to drive from California to Pennsylvania. Now we use various GPS technologies through a multitude of phone apps. Although the format may be different, the idea is the same. You must use a roadmap or plan if you are trying to get from point A to point B.

It does not matter what your personality type is, you need to create a plan, evaluate where you are, and map out the steps you need to take to get where you are trying to go. Don't worry, you don't have to do it completely on your own. You can talk to and study others who are where you want to be, or who have done what you want to do. Please keep in mind that no path in life is completely linear and, although you have a plan, everything will not go exactly as you envisioned it. Stay focused on your goal no matter what. Do not let anything stop you from accomplishing what is important to you.

Let's Get Focused!

We discussed the importance of setting goals and plans. However, they cannot be accomplished without focus! When I was in the church choir, a lady would always say, "Let's get focused!" Although I found her quite annoying, she was right in that if we wanted to learn the song, we needed to focus.

Focus is critical, especially when many distractions are competing for your attention. I know I can get easily distracted at times. I blame this on the advent of social media, which has contributed to our inability to focus on one thing for too long. We've grown accustomed to looking at this app and that app, reading one message and jumping to another when we receive a push notification. It is critical that we regain self-control and not let things that are unimportant distract us from our goals.

I once heard someone say, "You can wreck your car trying to swat at flies." I can attest to that. One summer day, I was driving, and a bug kept annoying me. I tried to swat it and before I knew it, I had barely missed a pole. After that experience, I developed a greater appreciation for the importance of focus. My goal was to reach the destination I was trying to reach at the time, but I let a trifling fly take me off my target. Oftentimes we run into many forms of flies: people, social media, problems, family, friends, drama, etc., but we cannot lose sight of what is most important! I understand that sometimes you may have something serious happen to you or to someone important to you. You may need to get off course for a while, but at some point, get back on the road.

Don't Give Up!

We've covered the importance of goal setting, planning, and staying focused. But you cannot do any of these things without determination – the hunger and drive to not give up! It includes focus but is more about pushing through and persevering no matter what. It is the attitude captured in mottos like: " I'm a winner and winners win" or "Go hard or go home!"

If you have lived long enough, you know that whenever you are trying to do something good there are always obstacles to push through. But you move forward and keep focused because what you are trying to accomplish is important to you.

It's kind of like trying to get into shape or losing weight. As you start your workout, you may feel pain or fatigue, but you know that it is part of the process to reach your goals. As you strain (and even moan) going through a grueling workout, you stay motivated because you know that there is a result that you desire, even though you cannot see it yet. Keeping that vision of the body or weight level that you are trying to attain pushes you through and that very act is a manifestation of determination.

Anything worth having requires a lot of hard work and determination, whereas things that are not worth having require very little work. Have you ever tried to maintain a lawn or grow and care for flowers? Did you have to do work to maintain them? Flowers are important things in life that we have to water, prune, and nurture. We must put work for them to bloom.

Weeds, on the other hand, just grow. We do not have to plant or prune them or put in any work for them to grow. Weeds are symbolic for the unimportant and distracting things that require no work to grow. Work hard and be relentless in killing them, as they are resilient. Show determination in overcoming the obstacles (or weeds) in your life to realize your goals (or flowers).

Keep pushing through the weeds of life to smell your flowers. Giving up is easy, but showing determination and perseverance is not. Someone once said that the key difference between successful and unsuccessful people is that successful people find ways to jump over their hurdles while unsuccessful people succumb to the hurdles. You can overcome the hurdles in your way through determination.

FOR REFLECTION

"Remember: Goal + Plan + Focus + Determination = Success."
~Carlos T. Carter

- What three goals do you want to accomplish this year?
- What can you do to make sure they are achieved?
- What obstacles stand in your way?
- How can you overcome these obstacles?
- What will you do to maintain your focus and resolve through the process of achieving your goals?

3 – ELEVEN KEYS TO LEADERSHIP
Nothing Great is Done Without Leadership

To be great, it is critical to know how to lead effectively. Great people have great ideas and want to do great things, but no one does anything great alone. I love the African proverb that says, "If you want to go fast, go alone. If you want to go far, go together." This proverb resonates with me as a Type A personality, often trying to keep things moving.

I have enough wisdom to know that if I try to do everything alone to move faster, there is no way I can achieve great things. Everything that I've done well was done with the support and encouragement of others. When you have a great team, it multiplies the strength of your leadership and empowers you to have a more profound impact on anything you do. My team at HCEF was amazing. There was no way that we could do such life changing work without that great team. I provided the high-level strategic direction/leadership, but they made everything happen.

I define leadership as the ability to influence others to follow you. If you say that you are leading and no one is following, then you are only taking a walk by yourself. Why people follow you determines whether your leadership is healthy or toxic.

Toxic leadership demands perfection. Toxic leaders bark commands are internally focused and lead with domination and control. This leadership is fear-based and rife with ego and insecurity. When you are secure in your own skin, you don't feel the need to dominate and control others. I agree with Bob Davids, when he wrote in his book, *Up the Organization*, that "The rarest commodity is leadership without ego."

Imagine being under leadership that does not seek to dominate and control but rather aims to motivate, inspire, empower, uplift, and bring out the best in your team to achieve a shared vision or goal! Healthy leadership is inspirational and externally focused on the people that you serve. Inspirational leaders are more inclined to ask questions and provide direction; they are willing to share power to empower others.

I am a big proponent of healthy inspirational leadership. I often coach other leaders because I believe there are too many managers and supervisors, but not enough inspirational leaders motivating, and inspiring people to become the best versions of themselves. If your leadership leaves people feeling marginalized, demoralized, and defeated, what does that say about you?

In thousands of comments on my viral blog posts, I was saddened to learn how many people have been subjected to toxic leadership. One woman, for example, talked about how her boss would holler at her, call her a liar, and repeatedly remind her that their VP title deserved respect. This lady spoke of her anxiety and fear of her boss and the need to pray in the restroom before going to her desk. Others spoke of the effects of these toxic work environments on their health and job performance.

When one experiences inspirational leadership, they feel empowered, energized, and ready to take on the world. In Daniel H. Pink's book *Drive*, he talks about his research and findings about what motivates people, and nowhere does he suggest bullying and control. He suggests things like giving people control over their destiny, a sense of purpose, mastery/challenge, empathy, etc.

When people think of leadership, they often think of a formal leadership role like a boss or leader of an organization or company, but we all have opportunities to lead and be led. The key thing that makes a leader is their ability to influence people. I remember a time when I was in between jobs. I expressed concern to my mentor that I did not have good leadership experience on my resume. He encouraged me to focus on influences I had in various roles. Even though I did not have direct reports, I was leading and influencing my team to accomplish shared goals. I had to motivate and encourage those around me when they were frustrated. That was a true epiphany for me, and I often encourage people who are not in formal leadership positions to see and leverage their ability to influence others.

Although I generally believe leaders are born, I also believe they are shaped by events and circumstances in life. Some believe leaders are made and there may be truth to that, but I believe you either have it or you don't. Author Bob Davids says that leaders are born not made. He goes on to liken leadership to being creative: you either have it or you don't. He and I would agree that leaders need training and development to take leadership to the next level.

To be a great leader, know when to lead and when to follow. Check your ego. Followership (ability to follow others) is important because you need to know when to leverage the team, and when to step back as the leader and let someone else lead in certain areas.

For me, working as a non-profit leader, there are times when I have to take a back seat to board members and staff who are experts in certain areas. For example, as a former executive director, I had to leverage the leadership and talents of my director of development who had twenty plus years of experience in fundraising. I used to defer to her expertise often.

11 Keys to Stand-up Leadership

These eleven keys are not the bible of leadership, but they are things I have observed that can facilitate productive leadership in work environments. If you can employ a few of these strategies, the state of leadership will be a better place for all. If you master at least three of these keys, you will be positioned to leverage your leadership to do great things!

1. Model the Way – "Don't talk about it, be about it!" Too often there are company missions and value statements, but do we see people in those companies living by them? As leaders, we must live the values. Although no one is perfect, people respect leaders who model the way. Your employees, or team should be able to look at your actions and see your values at work. The extent to which you model the way reveals your level of integrity.

2. Empathy/Kindness – When your mom used to say, "It is nice to be nice," her

advice is still relevant. The best leaders are kind and compassionate people. They often have high expectations for their teams but treat them with dignity and respect. Being kind will not only have a positive impact on employee morale and productivity, but also the bottom line. At the end of the day, Maya Angelou said, "people may not remember what you said or did, but how you made them feel." Being cruel and harsh is never productive.

3. Move Away from Positional Leadership – It is one thing to be a positional leader where people follow you because they must, but it is more important that people follow you because they know you care and are capable of moving the organization or team forward. I learned this from the author John Maxwell.

4. Catch People Doing Good – It is easy to criticize, but an effective way to motivate people is to reinforce good behavior. This practice will make your team feel more appreciated. Additionally, it will create a positive peer pressure for others to model. They will repeat behaviors that are rewarded and recognized.

5. Share Power – Good leaders empower their people by sharing power and enabling others to act. People want to have control over their destiny. When you share power, you will be given the opportunity to leverage followership. Micromanaging others is suffocating.

6. Manage Triggers - Leaders get frustrated like everyone else. Do your work and take the time to understand the internal things that impact your ability to lead effectively. When leaders operate more out of the "fight or flight" or triggered mode, they are less rational and less effective. Learn strategies to manage your emotions and triggers. This will position you to give your best and not allow your emotions to get hijacked. Further, you will make better decisions and avoid bad reactions.

7. Hire Leaders – Just because someone was a top accountant or top salesperson does not mean that they will be a good leader. Being able to manage a functional role does not mean you will be able to motivate others. Hire people with strong emotional intelligence who are good listeners. Choose candidates who can connect, motivate, and inspire others.

8. Coaching – I do believe that leaders are born, but they need coaching, mentorship, training, and development to take things to the next level. Make sure that you seek training and continuing education to lead more effectively.

9. Employee Input in Evaluations – Evaluations from leaders should not just be based on bottom line or general objectives. They should also include input from the direct reports of the leaders when possible. This is tricky because many employees fear retribution, but if done correctly, it can create greater accountability to leadership and healthy work environments.

10. It's Not About You! – True leaders are servants. Your ego, career, comfort, and needs do not come first. After your employees eat, you should be the one picking up their plates. When people know you care and are there to serve, they will knock down walls for you.

11. Know When to Follow – Great leaders know when they need to take a back seat and let their team members lead in a certain area. Enable others to act and empower them to become better leaders.

FOR REFLECTION
"True leaders are servants."
~Carlos T. Carter

- Where are some areas where you can grow as a leader?
- Which of these keys can you put into practice now?
- What are some areas where you need to share power or improve your followership?

"Faith is the substance of things hoped for and the evidence of things not seen."

Hebrews 11:1 (KJV)

4 – FAITH MATTERS!
The Power of Looking Beyond What You Can See!

Les Brown is my favorite motivational speaker. He was born into poverty and was told that he was illiterate. Now he is one of the most influential and successful motivational speakers in the world. I can give you numerous examples of people in tough situations who became successful. Of course, they worked hard and had to persevere through many challenges, but one thing that many had was faith.

Mr. Brown had a teacher who believed in him and supported him. This teacher had faith and believed that Mr. Brown was more than what he could see and more than what others saw in him. Despite his failures, Mr. Brown never gave up, because he believed that things would work out in the end.

Faith is important because it gives you peace, it creates hope for the future, and it gives you a reason to move forward and not give up! People have different perspectives on faith, whether it be faith in themselves or faith in God, etc. This chapter is not meant to proselytize or convert anyone into my belief system, but I believe it is important to share the impact faith has had on my life. If I were not to share this perspective, I would not be sharing my truth.

Faith Gives You Peace

I have always struggled with worry, but have you ever noticed that worry and peace are mutually exclusive and cannot coexist? I used to worry about fitting in. I worried about passing or failing a test. I worried about my kids. I worried about finding a job. I worried how I was going to send my middle son to college. I wasted time always worrying and had a sense of anxiety, but I cannot think of a single positive thing that came from this worrying.

At one point I was having a tough time and met with a counselor to discuss challenges in my personal life. He asked me to write a list of my concerns and worries. I took the time to write the list of five or six things and, after looking back none of those things came true. I was worked up and anxious for no reason. Does this sound familiar to you? Matthew 6:7 in the Bible says, "Can anyone of you by worrying add a single hour to your life?" (NIV). Worry is a time waster and can rob you of your peace!

Faith is the opposite of worry. It is the belief that things will be better. I believe that God will take care of things if I trust in Him. I would worry even when I used to say to myself that I had trust. I have learned to strengthen my faith by looking at the history of my Creator and knowing that He will provide for me and my family no matter what.

I believe now without a doubt like Les Brown and others, that all will be taken care of. Even if things do not go the way that I want, I know that all things will work to my good and something positive or a lesson will be learned from the negative experiences. This new perspective has given me more peace in my life and significantly less stress. Most importantly, I am at peace during challenging circumstances.

If you desire peace in your life, have the faith and trust that things will work out no matter what, this will give you a better quality of life and less stress, which is conducive to better health! Peace does not happen because of what is going on. It happens despite what is going on.

Hope For the Future

The wonderful thing about faith is that it not only gives peace, but it gives hope for the future! Just think about it: What if you based things on what you see now, how would that help you pursue your dreams? Although there are people who move forward without faith, I believe having faith helps you progress in a more empowered and productive fashion. For example, when I met my counselor, I was moving forward despite weak faith and worry.

My decision to put things in perspective and move forward in faith (with lofty expectations for the future) created an attitude shift. I became more positive and self-confident. At that point, I knew everything was going to work out. I was able to move forward in a more powerful and purposeful manner.

There are negative people in this world. Perhaps they have their reasons to be that way. I believe that if people had more faith, they would be more optimistic. They would have the confidence that good things are coming, no matter what was going on around them. I expect in faith that I will continue to prosper no matter what. That is why when people were feeling a sense of doom and gloom based on the outcome of the 2016 presidential election, I reminded myself that everything would work out. I would be lying if I said I did not have any concerns, but I put it into perspective and said to myself, *"My destiny is not determined by who is in the White House. My destiny is determined by my Creator who takes care of me. My future is bright, and I will continue to maintain hope for the future despite the persistent negative media or negativity of people."* I have faith that all will be well!"

Don't Give Up!

I know that you are not a quitter, but with faith you will really stay in the game. Several years ago, I started as a nonprofit leader. I was excited about my role, but boy does it require faith! There were challenges my people and I faced to move our organization forward. I continued to encourage myself and my team that we would have growing pains, but I let them know that we could move from good to great. I encouraged them to keep pushing. I told them, "This drive to move forward is not based on what I see, but on what I know because I am grounded in faith, and I want to encourage you to be grounded in the same way."

Through my faith, I know that things will always work out. I know that I do not have to give up when I have setbacks. I have the peace through faith that I can do all things and I want you to have the same faith. When haters tell you that you cannot do something, believe through faith that you can! Never give up. There is a larger plan you are trying to reach. As I wrote this chapter, Lord knows it was not easy, but I believed in faith that this book will impact and change peoples' lives in meaningful ways. I believe it will be prolific and sell a million copies. How do I know this? Through faith! Faith precedes greatness!

5 – THE POWER OF YES & NO
Two Words That Will Change Your Life!

Have you ever said yes to things that you really wanted to say no to? Did you wonder why you said yes? Was it because you thought the other person would be upset with you or you did not want to disappoint someone and just went along with the program? How did you feel afterwards? Probably not good, thinking something like: "Why did I not speak up?" or "Why do I always let others run over me?" This is a problem that many face for a variety of reasons. It is critical that you work to get to the point where you can leverage the power of "yes" and "no." If you want to achieve your goals, dreams, and the greatness that is within, you cannot avoid internal work!

A few years ago, I made the decision to write a book about the power of "yes" and "no." I was compelled to write because I had run into many people pleasers and saw the anguish that they faced trying to make others happy. I eventually realized that I could include those thoughts as a chapter in this book.

Don't get me wrong, I'm not against helping or pleasing others. Rather, I have a problem with people saying yes to other people's immediate needs or concerns while ignoring their own and impeding their ability to do things that are important for them. I believe in sacrificing for others, but at what point do you establish boundaries?

I know someone who doesn't handle her responsibilities but often expects others to have her back during a crisis. She then picks people she knows will always come to the rescue because they will rarely leverage their power to say "no." The sad thing is that these individuals want to say "no" but don't. Although this case is severe, I am certain that you have experienced this situation personally or have observed others who are not willing to establish boundaries. They won't say "no" or in the words of my late mother-in-law,"H2theNo!"

I've seen situations where someone has a lot on their plate, but constantly lets other people and things distract them. They may have to study for an exam or work on a project. They may be trying to meet a deadline. Nevertheless, they let someone convince them (or they convince themselves) that they should do something else. Unfortunately, the person goes along with it and later is stressed at the last minute trying to take care of what was most important, because they should have said "no." This whole predicament is the direct result of people-pleasing behavior and possibly a lack of discipline.

Stop People Pleasing

People pleasing leaves a person depleted and devalued. If you allow others to take advantage of you, they can sense your weakness and exploit it. It could be a boss, coworker, friend, relative, significant other. Learning to leverage the power of "yes" and "no" is critical if you want to achieve your goals and dreams with focus.

If you are always saying "yes" to others when you really want to say "no", you are saying "no" to what is important to you. Further, you are negating your voice. Not being able to say "yes" to what is important to you will impede your ability to tap into your greatness. This will occur because you are too preoccupied with the desires of others.

> "If you allow others to take advantage of you, they can sense your weakness and exploit it."

Get To the Root

If you want to fix any problem, you need to get to the root of it. Lord knows that I am not a psychologist or psychoanalyst, but I believe that our inability to say "no" may be rooted in our childhood. Some people may have dealt with rejection as a child or a teenager and people pleasing has been a way to fit in or be accepted. For me, it has felt like I did not fit in at times, but I was fortunate not to get too caught up in pleasing people. I realized that it would not make much sense and was not too shy to say no. I have been guilty of pleasing people from the perspective of not being honest about who I was to fit in. In essence, that was people pleasing.

There are people who may have grown up in a household with alcoholism or other dysfunction and learned to do what it takes to please others to protect themselves or to try to hold things together. Maybe you have been bullied and that affected your self-esteem and the need to please people. Whatever the reason, do your work to get to the root of the issue. In the words of Iyanla Vanzant, a well-known inspirational speaker and life coach, "You cannot fix what you won't face."

Getting to the root of your issues is critical if you want to discover your greatness! Talk to close friends or a therapist to help you. I went to counseling to work through some of the traumas in my life. Counseling allowed me to grow as a person and as a professional. If this level of work scares you, it is okay. You can push through it. One of my favorite quotes from Les Brown is: "Do what is easy and life will be hard; do what is hard and life will be easy."

        Realize That You Are Important

Some experiences in life may have diminished your perception of your value. You may have had a parent or someone else tell you that you were worthless or that you will never be anything or even had job situations that diminish you. You have value that is not dictated by your salary, education, social standing, race, gender, sexual orientation, etc. You don't have to prove your value to anyone. I believe that God has imputed value in everyone, and He does not make any junk! Starting today, look at yourself in the mirror and say, "I am important, I matter, and I have a purpose!" These words of affirmation will support you as you work to assert your power to say "yes" and "no" to what is important to you!

Recognize and Own Your Power

You may be struggling with the ability to leverage your power, but if you realize that you already have it, you can acknowledge it and embrace it.

At times I look at social media when I should be doing something else, and I stay on longer than I should. I am learning to leverage my power and say: "No, you do not have to keep searching. You can get off the internet and do other things that are more important." This is an example of power that is not always being fully utilized. You have the power, acknowledge, and activate it! Try not to be a people pleaser. Leverage your power to say "yes" to things that are important to you!

FOR REFLECTION
*"You have the power,
acknowledge and activate it!"*
~Carlos T. Carter

- How does people pleasing affect your ability to accomplish your goals and dreams?
- What are you willing to do today to leverage your power to say "yes" or "no?"

6 – HEALTHY & HOLISTIC LIVING
You Can Be Great When You Are Whole

Say "yes" to healthy and holistic living. Daily life is filled with "hustle and bustle." Working parents try to juggle the demands of kids and work. Single parents struggle to do the jobs of two parents, and it can take a toll! I grew up in a single-parent home and have no idea how my mother managed to do it all! Even people who are not in a relationship are pressed with the day-to-day struggles of trying to balance life's demands. How do we take care of ourselves in the process?

I have heard that we are one of the most successful generations, but how is success defined? Is it defined by people who run from task to task and place to place but never take care of themselves? Is it defined by the busiest and most stressed-out person with a wad of money? We all have careers, family, etc., to take care of, but what happens if we don't take care of ourselves? What happens if you ignore your health and well-being? Nothing will be good until you focus on healthy and holistic living.

Healthy and holistic living means focusing on the whole you, making sure that you are taking care of your mind, body, and spirit. Take care of yourself now and you'll be less of a burden later.

Take Care of Your Health

According to the National Institute of Health, more than two thirds or 68.8% of U.S. adults are considered overweight or obese. This is an alarming statistic, but not completely shocking as there is constant chatter on the news about the American struggle with the bulge. This problem contributes to many other health problems and issues that can be avoided. I'm not trying to criticize anyone, we all have our vices, but the fact is that this is taking away from our quality of life and longevity.

Take care of yourself. Your health cannot be ignored because you are busy with other things. I want to encourage you to eat right and go to regular doctors' appointments. How can you live a good life if your health is failing? You might be fine now, but if you don't take care of your body and your health, you will have hell to pay later!

Healthy does not necessarily mean "skinny." There are plenty of unhealthy skinny people. My father was skinny, but unfortunately, he passed away from lung cancer at the age of fifty-eight. I wish he was still around. I don't want your loved ones to have regrets about your being gone too soon because you failed to give your health the attention it deserves.

Health is important if you want to make sure that you are living and giving your personal best. How can you be at your best if you are feeling lethargic? How can you be your best if you feel bad about yourself because you are out of shape? How can you be your best if you are not eating right and neglecting yourself? I implore you to start. Meet with your doctor to get some guidance on what will work for you. Meet with a personal trainer, nutritionist, or any reputable person to see what can help you get on track. You owe it to yourself, what are you waiting for? If you are already taking care of yourself keep up the good work!

Find An Outlet

Balance is important, and I would be lying if I said that I have achieved it. I do know that it is important to find things that you love to do. This can help you take your mind off work and the daily pressures of life. Destress and have a good time. I would ask that you join me in this pursuit. I 'm sure that we'll both be better for it.

Sometimes we have difficulty relaxing. A few things that really help me destress include weightlifting, working out, running, dancing, karaoke, writing, and creating. If you have not found an outlet, find your thing, and make sure it helps your mind in a healthy way. Discover or rediscover what allows you to totally relax and escape the daily grind. The funny thing is that I am probably not qualified to talk about finding an outlet – I do not do this enough. I realize the importance of it and will commit to leveraging positive outlets more this year. Having outlets will serve as a recharge and an escape. If you keep a machine running all the time, it may eventually overheat and wear down!

You deserve a break!

Making A Spiritual Connection

I talked about faith in Chapter four and how it gives peace and hope. I want to talk more about the importance of having some sort of spiritual connection. It puts my mind at ease and connects me to something larger than myself. My faith helps to complete me. I'm not going to push my beliefs on you as this is not the purpose of this book, but I do want to tell you that you are missing something if you do not have a spiritual connection.

Having a spiritual connection helps to fill that hole or God Spot (the need to connect with a higher being and purpose) that we all have. We were all created to believe in and worship something greater than us. Look at various

cultures around the world and you will see that most have a religion or belief system.
For me, it is not just custom or convenience, it is part of my being and essential for holistic living. I believe we are mind, body, and spirit and if you ignore the spiritual piece, you will not be complete.

I implore you to commit to healthy holistic living and take care of your mind, body, and spirit. Take care of your health, have an outlet, and make a spiritual connection. These things will complete you and help you create a healthy and holistic life for yourself!

A Few Pointers for Good Self-Care

Starting today, make time to take care of yourself! You don't necessarily need to take a trip to the mall or whip out your credit card to engage in self-care! Keep it simple, keep it fun, and make sure that it refreshes your mind, body, and spirit!

1. Schedule It – We all are busy and can neglect our well-being. Prioritize your self-care activities on your calendar and stick to them.

2. Keep it Simple – Self-care may include a vacation but can also be a staycation. It is where you can unplug your social media and

plug into offline relationships. Having deeper and healthier connections to family and friends is always a good part of self-care.

3. Enjoy It – Try doing things you enjoy. If you don't like going to the gym, ride a bike, do yoga, or engage in another activity. Part of self-care may include having a good laugh – we all need more of those for sure! It could include dancing and listening to good music! Anybody who knows me well knows that I love to dance!

FOR REFLECTION
"I implore you to commit to healthy holistic living and take care of your mind, body, and spirit."
~Carlos T. Carter

- What are some challenges that affect your ability to be more balanced?
- What can you do today to promote more balance in your life?

7 – LEAD WITH PASSION & PURPOSE
Understanding Your "What' and "Why"

I recently wrote a LinkedIn article called "Get Out," not to be confused with the Jordan Peele blockbuster movie, but it certainly had the same sentiment. It was read and liked over one hundred thousand times and shared thousands of times and, as a result, doubled the number of my followers. I am not mentioning this article to brag (maybe a little-LOL) but to stress the point of understanding your "what" and "why" and the importance of leading with passion and purpose!

In my "Get Out" article, I tell a story of a friend who was trapped in a job that was misaligned with his passion and purpose. He did not feel fulfilled, valued, or appreciated and decided to get out as it was taking a toll on him emotionally and physically. He wanted to do something that he was passionate about. Just like in the movie, my friend needed to escape his job. He was losing himself. I thought the article was decent, but had no clue that it would go viral, or that people could relate to his story. A lot of people are not walking in their purpose.

You hear people talk about following your passion, and it becomes trite. Nevertheless, it is still important. Growing up, people asked me what I wanted to be when I grew up. The words "passion" and "purpose" were never mentioned. I thought of careers that interested me, but passion and purpose? No!

My first real introduction to personal purpose was reading *The Purpose Driven Life* by Pastor Rick Warren in 2002. Everybody was reading this book, not just church folks. It took the world by storm and sold more than thirty million copies as of 2019. It was translated in more than 85 languages. When I read this book with my church, I found it fascinating. It got me thinking about what I was created to do, but those thoughts quickly evaporated as I continued pursuing my career as a banker and climbing the corporate ladder. At that point, I was not in tune with my passion and purpose.

I always knew I wanted to do more. Some of the people I worked with at various banks could see that as well. One person at work told me that I was going to do great things one day. Others would say, "You are too smart to do this current job and you should be doing something greater." Still, others would say "You really care about people, there is something else that you should be doing." Those words were flattering, but I really did not know what else I wanted to do besides banking.

After my various job losses, I started thinking more about my passion and purpose. Heck, when you don't have a job, you have a lot more time to think about what you want to do and with greater urgency. When you have bills to pay, you need to find ways to put food on the table. Unemployed, I reflected more on my interest in becoming a nonprofit leader and motivational speaker. Both areas help people realize their potential, and I believe that was part of my mission, passion, and purpose.

Not long after I transitioned from banking into a nonprofit consultant role, I met another nonprofit leader and founder Julius Boatwright at Inclusive Voices. This is an event where we were table conversationalists with four hundred other people. A conversationalist leads the discussion about anything that was on their mind. After the event, Julius and I decided to meet for coffee. We talked about our backgrounds and organizations, but Julius said something that was profound. Before he introduced what he did, he said, "I want to not only talk about what I do, but why I do it!"

That floored me. I had never heard anyone talk like that. I knew I was passionate about what I was doing but had not totally contemplated my "why" or explained my "why" to people. I would never speak or think the same way again. He also suggested that I watch the "Start With Why" Ted Talk from Simon Sinek. I have watched it many times since.

My why – I want everyone to discover their value, passion and purpose and the greatness that is within. I believe that when you walk in your passion and purpose and live authentically that you will discover your greatness and do great things. My mission is to help people discover their greatness.

My what – the work I do as a nonprofit leader through various programs that connect people and resources that will help them get out of poverty and become the best versions of themselves. Through my motivational speaking my "what" includes: training, videos, coaching, speaking, encouraging, and finding ways to uplift and inspire people to pursue their passion and purpose and their greatness. Your "what" is important, as it is the actions and steps you will take to carry out your "why."

If you plan to lead with passion and purpose, you need to understand your why. If I say that I am a motivational speaker and nonprofit leader, I need to understand my "why" first and make sure my "what" is in sync with my "why"! Your activities and your profession should line up with your purpose.

What Excites You?

What things do you always think about or talk about? You may even want to check with some of your friends and family and ask what they think you are excited about. You may learn something new about yourself or affirm what you already knew about yourself. No matter what, this exercise will help give you some focus around your passion.

What Problems Do You Want to Solve in The World?

When I was consulting for a local school, I learned about a new approach to careers. This approach encourages you to choose a career that meets your interest and at the same time considers what problems you want to solve in the world. I believe that many students have low self-esteem, underestimate their value, and don't have a sense of purpose. These are problems that I am trying to solve, and I do it through my nonprofit leadership and my motivational speaking, articles, posts, etc. You need to figure out what problems you want to solve if you do not know it already. This is a big clue to your passion and purpose and understanding your "why" and finding your "what."

What Are Your Talents or What Are You Good At?

What are the things you do well? Are you good with your hands? Are you good at solving problems? Are you good at speaking or talking to people? Do you have other talents? You may even want to ask your friends and family as they may recognize gifts that you don't. Everyone has gifts and talents, and some are undiscovered. Write down and evaluate your talents. This is critical as one can be passionate about something and not have the talent to back it up. For example, you may say that you are passionate about football, and want to play, but if you are not athletic and can barely throw a football, that may not be a good passion to pursue. You can always be a spectator. Just make sure your passion and talents line up, otherwise, it may be an exercise in futility. When your passion collides with your talent and gifts, great things happen!

What Do People See in You?

Understand what makes you special. We all have things that others see as special about us. It could be a talent but could just be an essence that sets one apart. You may be likable, encouraging, empathetic, etc. You may have the type of personality that lights up a room. This thing that makes you special may be a clue to leverage your passion.

What Does the World Need That God Has Put in You?

I believe that God has put something in each of us that the world needs. What is it about you that the world needs? There is something about you that can be used to change the world. For me, I believe that it is my love for humanity and a calling to encourage others. For you, it may be something else. No matter what, there is only one you and you were created for a purpose, as I do not believe that God creates junk. You are beautifully and wonderfully made and there is something in you that the world needs.

FOR REFLECTION
"Lead with passion and purpose!"
~Carlos T. Carter

- What excites you?
- What problems do you want to solve in the world?
- What does the world need that God has put in you?
- What are your talents and gifts and what are you good at?
- What do people see in you?

8 – DON'T SETTLE
Committed to Growth

Have you ever met anyone who just seems to be stuck? Someone in a place of closed-mindedness and no growth? I've seen people who are walking around in daily mundane circles – with no curiosity or ambition. The sad thing is that we all have potential, but if we don't seek growth and opportunities to learn and stretch ourselves, we will never realize our true potential or become the best version of ourselves.

Realizing Your Personal Best

Continuous learning is a great way to realize your personal best. I have always been inquisitive, so much so that my mom bought encyclopedias to try to keep up with and manage my inquisitiveness. I have always been hungry to understand the world around me. Now, when I need to know something, I can Google it or find a book.

I am sure I am not the only person who was inquisitive as a child. Unfortunately, as people grow into adulthood, they often get into complacent life routines. They stop seeking information to promote curiosity and growth. Never stop seeking new knowledge and opportunities for growth! Someone once said, "If something is not growing, it is dying." Yes, we all must go at some point. While you are still here, keep seeking opportunities to grow and propel yourself to be your best.

When I started leading HCEF, I read books on leadership and observed other leaders. I wanted to be the best leader possible. As I do my motivational speaking, I continue to seek information and learn from other great speakers. Every day I am working to become the best speaker possible. A few years ago, I took a Strengths Finder Test, and my top listing was "Learner." I was surprised, but it is consistent with my constant pursuit of knowledge and understanding that began as a child.

Discovering New Places

Constant learning will take you to new places. This is accomplished through increasing your knowledge from reading or consuming information in different forms. This only occurs when you are willing to physically do things that you have not done before. When you stretch yourself, you will learn about other people, cultures, and backgrounds. That entire experience will literally take you mentally and physically to another place, and through that experience you will be learning and growing.

> "Constant learning will take you to new places."

This experience of going to new places can be scary. I have mentioned some of my experiences. I recently went through a leadership program, and I was sent to a ranch with people from all over the country. I had never been on a ranch, let alone in the Sonoma Valley. I had to share personal things with people I did not know. It forced me to push through some uncomfortable situations, but in the end, I felt like I really grew. My growth would never have happened without a willingness to learn and leave my comfort zone. I have new friends and new perspectives, and I am better for it.

Keep Yourself Relevant

Seeking knowledge will help you stay relevant. If you don't innovate, you'll become irrelevant. I want to tell you about a couple I know who manage their own business. They are the nicest people in the world, and I am fond of them. However, they run a business where they type everything on a typewriter. For my younger readers, a typewriter is a machine that people used back in the day to type letters and other things. Typewriters were discontinued in the late eighties or early nineties.

Typewriters are not as sophisticated as a computer. There is no backspace which allows you to delete. You cannot save automatically.

With a typewriter, what you type must be corrected with correction tape or white out. My fear for my friends is that they will not be able to compete with other business operators. They are inefficient due to their use of technology that is more than three decades behind.

When you are stuck in the past, your ability to thrive and keep up with what is going on today is limited. Many things are timeless, especially when it comes to values. I want to encourage you to be aware of and open to new technology, ideas, and information. This will keep you relevant with your business clients, your approach, and outlook on life. There is nothing worse than someone who is stuck in the past and unable to move forward because they have become irrelevant.

FOR REFLECTION

"Greatness awaits you! Intentionally seek knowledge and opportunities to grow."
~Carlos T. Carter

- Where are some areas where you need to increase your knowledge?
- What are you willing to commit to today to help you grow and achieve your goals and dreams?

9 – TAKE RISKS
Don't Let Anything Stop You from Pursuing Your Dreams

What is holding you back from your dreams? If you want to do anything worthwhile in life, you have to be willing to take risks. Go for it!

I was often crippled by fear when I was growing up. I was raised with the worldview that "anything can go wrong." I thought I had to play it safe. I used to think, *"What if I do this and that happens? What if I do that and this happens? What would people think? How would I look?"* I often wanted to try out for various sports, but let fear stop me. I have often regretted that decision. Over the years, I have realized that to do anything worthwhile, I have to be willing to take risks. Risks are often equal to rewards because they challenge and stretch you.

Risk Equals Reward

As a former banker and finance minor (not major-LOL), I know a little about investing. When you invest but are not willing to take risks, you may be less likely to lose, but the return on your investment and potential for gain is limited. I am certainly not against more conservative investments with a low risk profile. They are necessary at certain points in your life, especially when you are about to retire and need to preserve your nest egg. However, taking risks gives you a fuller and more satisfying life experience. Find opportunities to put yourself out there despite your fears. When I first started seriously creating motivational videos, writing articles, speaking, etc., I was nervous. I didn't know what people would think and I was afraid of failing. I told myself, *"This is important to me to accomplish my goals and dreams and I am willing to push past my comfort zone."*

Although I have made some mistakes along the way, I have continued to get better and believe that the return on the investment I made has been great. I especially see this manifest in the many comments I receive from around the world. People often tell me that my inspirational messages have made a positive impact on their lives and encouraged them to do things that they never would have done. Don't be afraid to take a risk – the rewards are great!

Taking Risks Will Challenge and Stretch You

When I received the courage to start my motivational business, at times I was scared out of my mind. Remember I told you about being contacted by the Woodland Hills School District? The assistant superintendent wanted me to inspire them to remember the reason they chose to teach.

Ironically, I had several other presentations to do that month and felt stressed and pressured.

The level of stress and fear I had before this presentation was unbearable. I was completely out of my comfort zone. I knew I would need to be vulnerable in my presentation to make a strong impact.

I came up with the title: *How My Teacher Changed My Life.* I shared personal and vulnerable childhood experiences and I explained how Dr. Toliver helped get me where I am today, despite my challenges. My goal was to leave the teachers energized, inspired, and renewed. In the end, I grew in the process and became more confident as a speaker. This was one of the proudest moments in my life. I gave them everything that I had, and they received it. I leveraged not only my speaking voice but my singing voice as well to get my message across. I knew that I took a big risk and there was a chance they would reject me, but they received me and my message with open arms.

In addition to the speaking engagement, the Woodland Hills School District team asked me to do a leadership workshop for twenty principals and administrators. I had never done such a workshop. I fretted about whether I would do a good job. When the assistant superintendent invited me, I tried to get out of it, but she was encouraging to me.

My title for the workshop was *"Empowered and Passionate Leadership: Becoming the Leader Everyone Wants to Follow."* Although I was apprehensive about this presentation, I prepared by interviewing many educators and principals for insight on the profession and to really get a sense of the challenges these individuals face.

On the day of the workshop, I was still nervous, but once it came time to present, I jumped in, and the nervousness melted away like butter. I was able to really connect and engage with the administrators and was surprised at how freely and openly they shared their challenges as leaders. We discussed ways for them to overcome many of their hurdles. I conducted a survey afterwards and received favorable reviews. This was another growth experience for me and underscored the power of taking risks. I would be lying if I said that I am never nervous or scared, but these experiences have helped me become a better speaker and have given me the courage to do bigger and better things.

You Want to Have a Life of No Regrets

One of my favorite quotes that emphasizes the burden of regret on our lives is from author Robert Hastings. He says, "It isn't the burdens of today that drive men mad. It is the regrets over yesterday and the fear of tomorrow. Regret and fear are twin thieves who rob us of today."

As I write this chapter, I am forty-eight years old. I cannot waste my years left on this earth having regrets and feeling sorry for myself because I did not take the opportunity to truly live my life, be fully who I am, or do everything that I have been created to do. To be honest, I am not the best at living in the moment. I am always thinking about the next thing that can be done. When I come to the end of my life, I do not want to think about all the things I could have or should have done but did not do because I was afraid. I want to enjoy every day fully and never want to be robbed by fear and regret. I want you to live your life to its fullest. Life is too short to let anything stop you from pursuing your dreams. If you fail, it is not the end of the world.

FOR REFLECTION

"Success is not final; failure is not fatal: it is the courage to continue that counts!"
~Winston Churchill

- What risks are you afraid to take?
- Will you have regret not taking these risks?
- What are three things you can do to move past your fear of taking risks?

10 – LIVE TO GIVE!
It's Not All About You!

We live in a capitalistic society that can at times be overly focused on individuals at the expense of the greater good. I am not against personal success, but if your success and all you do is focused on you, that is not very fulfilling. I believe true fulfilment comes when what you do helps uplift others. When I think about people like Dr. Martin Luther King Jr., who endured racism and persecution and ultimately lost his life to help others, I think of how he is an example of someone who lived to give. You don't have to put your life on the line for others, but if you want a fulfilling life, live to give!

You Will Live

You may live a "good life" where you work at a successful career, travel often, live in a big home, drive a fancy car, or eat at any restaurant you want. Doing things that you enjoy is great, and I like doing the same, but if everything is just about you and your happiness and needs, then your life will become hollow. I've seen people with all the success of life but not much focus on helping or giving to others. Once they retired and looked back on life, they felt unfulfilled and were seeking something to fulfill them. If you invest in only yourself, the return is not as robust as when you invest in others.

I spent roughly eighteen years in the banking industry and for the most part liked many of my jobs. Yet at times, I knew that something was missing. Although I liked the money I made, I often felt like an outsider. Most of my coworkers did not share my values or passion to empower and serve others. I often found opportunities to serve on boards, mentor kids, and speak to kids about pursuing their dreams and financial literacy. I found these experiences challenging and rewarding. Although I did not necessarily try to analyze why I felt good about serving and helping others, I knew it was fulfilling to make a positive impact on others. I had a longing to make not only money, but also a greater impact on the world. This desire led to my transition into the nonprofit world.

Even with these great experiences, I did not really feel like I was living until I was in my forties. By that time, I had started to immerse myself in activities where I felt like I was making a greater impact on my people and humanity. When I worked at a school, I felt a sense of belonging and connectedness I had never felt in the banking industry.

The funny thing is that people would always tell me they noticed how I care about people and was always positive. I remember one of my bosses saying: "You should do something in the community." These people could see my passion for helping people even more than I did. I believe that they could see my passion and how I was at my best when I was doing things to uplift others.

My greatest experiences with giving and helping others were when I started becoming more serious about my motivational speaking, videos, articles, and blogs. I remember a leader telling me, "I look to your motivational posts to make it through the week." That really made me feel good that she valued the content that I was sharing, but more importantly that it was having a positive impact on her life. Moments like these help me feel alive, and it is only because I have chosen to help and pour into others which in turn, refills me. I truly believe that when you pour out what is inside you, God continues to fill you up. If you keep it inside, it becomes stale.

I would often see one of my colleagues outside of our building smoking a cigarette. I would jokingly holler at her, "Put the cigarette down." When she would see me, she would try to hide it and I would say, "It's okay, you will quit. Tomorrow is a new day; you will start then." My experience with this young lady affirms the fulfillment you receive helping others. Recently, she said I have been the primary motivator for her to quit. I hope that her health is the primary reason, but I felt good that I could help.

If you are at a point in your life where you do not feel fulfilled, it may be because your life is too much about yourself and not enough about helping others.

You Will Be Richly Blessed

Although the focus of living is to give, it is not about doing things just to get something for yourself - that is a natural consequence. Living to give is driven by the principle of sowing and reaping. If you sow seeds or invest good things in others, they will benefit others. They will in turn benefit you as well.

I've watched some of the people I have mentored grow. One time I was in a community Bible study and the men were sharing different experiences. A young man came up to me and thanked me for everything that I had done for him growing up. His mom had substance abuse issues and he and his brother, to be honest, were sometimes out of control. I would try to listen, talk, and guide the oldest brother, let's call him "Sam."

I never told anyone about it until now, but when school was about to start, I learned that these boys needed school clothing. I asked them their sizes, went shopping, and bought them school clothes. I knew how important going to school looking presentable is, especially since other kids can be cruel. I felt truly blessed to discreetly help him and his brother. I know sometimes parents can feel ashamed if they are not able to do things for their kids. I didn't want to upset their mother, but I think she was appreciative. I could empathize with the boys not having new clothes. I remembered my mom doing her best but not having a lot of resources to buy me new clothes. Therefore, when Sam thanked me years later and said that I have always been like a father to him, that truly touched my heart deeply and yes, I felt blessed.

I don't want to come across as self-righteous. I can be a selfish creature at times as well. If you don't believe me, just ask my wife! We all need attitude adjustments and to get refocused on what is most important, but I truly believe that when you invest in others, they will be blessed and so will you! Since I have dedicated my life to serving others, I now have a level of fulfillment in my life that is unparalleled by any other time in my life. Money and things can never give me the same level of joy and fulfillment as my decision to serve others. This goes with the concept of what you sow is what you reap.

You Will Bless Others and Leave a Legacy That Will Keep on Giving

My mom has always been a giving person, I've seen her give her last to help others in need or crisis. I've watched her help young people in need. I remember one of my sisters' friends having trouble at home and needing a place to stay and my mom took her in. I remember times when relatives fell on hard times, and she would not hesitate to accommodate them. Some were better guests than others. No matter what, she always gives to others.

I am sure the people she has helped are grateful to her for taking them in and supporting them. She was a blessing to those in need. I have never asked my mother what motivated her to give but based on what I know about her and the many challenges she faced including brief homelessness, I know that she does it because she knows what it's like to be in desperate situations. She specifically told me that when she was a young mother, her mother put her out of the house with two young children, including me. Thank God for the neighbors who took us in. That is what being a good neighbor is all about.

When you help others, that gift keeps on giving. It makes the world a better place for all. Just like in the example with my mom, someone helped her in her time of need. That act of kindness encouraged her and she continues to do the same for others. This perpetuates a legacy that keeps on giving. I believe it has influenced my desire to be a blessing to others.

As you go about your day, remember to find opportunities to be a blessing to others. In the process you not only will be a blessing to them, but you will also be blessed and live a life that is truly fulfilling.

FOR REFLECTION
"When you help others, the gift keeps giving."
~Carlos T. Carter

- What talents and resources do you have that could help others?
- How would you like to make a difference in the world?
- Starting today, what can you do to do more for others?

11 – THE PURSUIT OF EXCELLENCE
Advancing Toward Your Personal Best

When you think of excellence or commitment to excellence, what comes to mind for you? Is it perfectionism? In the dictionary, excellence is defined as "the fact or state of excelling, superiority, eminence." When I look at the word 'excellence,' the adjective form is "possessing outstanding quality or superior merit, remarkably good. My definition of excellence is always giving your best or working towards giving your best. Excellence is not perfectionism or trying to be perfect, which can lead to marginalization of yourself and others. I believe that people should constantly strive to give their best and help bring out the best in others without falling into the trap of perfectionism.

I learned this Aristotle quote from my good friend Cassandra Brently: "You are what you repeatedly do, therefore, excellence is not an act but a habit." I met Cassandra when I was a consultant at Nazareth Prep (formerly known as Holy Family Academy). She was the Director of Admissions, and I was acting director prior to her arrival. Together, we worked very hard to create a more efficient and effective admissions department with the goal of recruiting students to take advantage of the great internship and educational opportunities at the school.

She had the Aristotle quote as her email signature and was committed to excellence.

Everything that she did, she did well, and was instrumental to building out the admissions office, increasing school brand awareness, and boosting student recruitment. I would see the marketing materials she created and how diligently she worked. She always made sure everything was completed with a high standard.

Although I am a big fan of commitment to excellence and high standards, I believe that it is equally important to try and avoid perfectionism. I have sometimes fallen into this trap, and it is counterproductive. I can remember times when I was demoralized because I made a mistake, and it was sometimes crippling. I can remember a time when I was performing and did not sing the song to the standard of my liking. I just ruminated on it. It was holding me back from giving my best, because I was too hard on myself and expecting perfection. I can think of times in jobs where I did not do something as well as I thought I should and just dwelled on it too long. Nothing productive came out of that approach.

This type of crippling perfectionism is never good and sometimes can stem from deeper issues with parents or others who have had very high expectations for us as children or may just be a part of our personality type. I am not saying that we should not try to do things well. Instead, we should allow room for imperfection, knowing that we are not perfect and should focus on continually making progress and doing the best we can. All of this begs the questions: How can you give your best and bring out the best in others without falling into perfectionism? What does a healthy pursuit of excellence look like?

How To Give Our Best

I believe that you can give your best without falling into the trap of perfectionism. If you are a baseball player looking to hit a home run every time, that is probably unrealistic. I am no baseball player or expert, but know the odds are slim to hit a home run every time at bat. If you are a competitor, you will still do your part to win the game. You will strive to get on base and eventually to home plate. You will do your best to help your teammates score and stop your opponents from scoring. In order to contribute to your team it is critical that you train and do what it takes to improve your skill. Your hard work and determination will create opportunities for more home runs. It will empower you to help your team win. You will not hit a home run every time and that is okay. Like the baseball player example, in life you must pursue progress and practice your craft to progress.

As you pursue excellence, work to get better and do the best that you can! Sometimes you will fall short and that is okay. You should not expect to be perfect every time. It's simply not possible and futile. I stumbled across this quote on perfectionism by Anne Wilson Schaef: "Perfectionism is self-abuse of the highest order." I wish I had learned that quote many years ago, but, as they say, better late than never. Knowledge is power and if you apply it, it is even more powerful. Just know that you give your best simply by making progress every day. Seeking to learn from mistakes and gaining knowledge will help you become the best you can be.

You can avoid perfectionism by simply realizing that you are not perfect. Give yourself some grace knowing that when you are being overly hard on yourself, you are being counterproductive and preventing yourself from becoming the best version of yourself. When you make mistakes or things fall short, focus on the positive and celebrate what you did right while at the same time finding ways to make progress each day to reach your goal. And if you never get things to the level that you want, that is okay, because you are not perfect!

How To Bring Out the Best in Others

You bring out the best in others by simply encouraging them. You must help them see their value even if they don't see it themselves. I don't focus on trying to catch my team members doing something wrong. It is more important that I intentionally celebrate when they do something right. I know my team probably believes that I have high standards for them. At the same time, they know I don't tear them down for mistakes.

When I started in my role as the leader of HCEF, I had an intelligent employee who had a few things to learn. She was not responsible for the total budget, but needed to master the budget for her programs, and I challenged her to take on that task. I could tell that she was nervous, but I always tried to reassure her that she could do it and made myself available for support and to address any questions that she had. I intentionally provided this challenge to her, because I knew that she could do it if she stretched herself a little. Although there were moments of worry and occasional mistakes, she has risen to the challenge and really helped improve overall budgeting and process in her program. She has received several promotions and seems a lot more confident. The main reason I believe that she was able to do this is because she is smart. Additionally, it helped that I intentionally created a supportive environment while providing room for mistakes or imperfections.

If you want to bring out the best in others, you must see the best in them and set high expectations. Your expectations need to be realistic and achievable. You want to ensure that you are not trapping people into the bondage of perfectionism, where nothing is ever good enough. Give them room to make mistakes.

As a young father, I made the mistake of putting too much pressure on my kids and did not always give them the grace and reassurance I should have. Although I did not reflect on it at the time, in my mind I was thinking that I wanted the best for them. I had high expectations, because they are smart and talented, but the effect sometimes was opposite my intention. My approach sometimes made them feel like they were not good enough or could not live up to my high expectations. I have since made some adjustments. Though this perfectionistic outlook is part of dominant American and other cultures, it is often toxic. According to Kenneth Jones and Tema Okun, authors of "White" Organizational Culture, mistakes often reflect badly on the person as opposed to being seen for what they are as simply mistakes. I made these mistakes early in my parenting approach, but I am deliberate now to make every effort not to subject others to this and I hope you will do the same.

Healthy Excellence

Healthy excellence means working toward progress without falling into the trap of perfectionism. It is knowing that you are never going to be perfect and that is okay. However, getting back to Aristotle's quote: "You are what you repeatedly do, therefore, excellence is not an act but a habit."

I urge you to remember at least one thing from here: perfectionism is not healthy and should be avoided at all costs! Instead, focus on giving your best and not beating up yourself and others when that doesn't happen. Understand that no one is perfect and that is okay. Greatness will truly await you when you pursue excellence instead of perfectionism!

FOR REFLECTION

"Seeking to learn from mistakes and gaining knowledge – that's what will help you become the best you can be."
~Carlos T. Carter

- What does excellence mean to you?
- What can you do to give excellence and avoid the pitfalls of perfectionism?
- Are there areas in your life where you need to give yourself grace? List some things you can do to be kinder to yourself.
- What can you do to bring out healthy excellence in others?

12 – VOTE FOR YOU!
It's Time to Cast a Vote for Yourself

According to Author Levi Lesco, the average American spends five hours a week on their phone. That's a third of a day, which is a lot of time wasted. I hate to say it, but I am in that category more often than I want. I continue to discipline myself to break away from this addiction to invest in more productive activities that will contribute to my personal growth and well-being. Yes, I said it, it's an addiction. When we are on our phone looking at likes, shares, waiting for comments, they bring us great pleasure. Dopamine is released and when we are away from our phones, the brain is stressed and produces cortisol, also known as a "fight-or-flight" hormone. As I was writing this passage, I was tempted to look at my phone instead of writing, but I had to resist the temptation and put my time into achieving the goal of completing this book!

Although phones are nice, I believe there is a better investment of our time in ourselves. Too often, you may invest in things that are not important, but when are you going to invest in yourself? Don't get me wrong, as a nonprofit leader and inspirational speaker and writer, I am all about investing in others. How can we invest in others if we are not willing to invest in ourselves? Starting today, it is time to vote for you by investing in yourself! This choice will put you in a better position to help others. Most importantly, you'll discover your passion and purpose to become the best version of yourself.

Get Focused on What Is Important

There are many things competing for your time: phones, people, work, family, etc. Make time to take inventory and prioritize what is most important and focus on the key activities that are of most importance, which will take you from where you are to where you want to be. For example, if you have a personal priority to spend more time with your family, there will be work demands and other things that pop up, but you will need to set boundaries to make sure that you don't let those things trump this priority. You may have to do things like refuse to look at emails after a certain time or commit to not taking calls while you are with family

Only you know what things are most important for you, and you must take time to think about what they are. If you fail to get focused or even know what is important, you will look up one day and realize that you have not been able to accomplish things that are important to you. Things that are most important are the things that matter most to you and have serious implications for the now and the future if you do not prioritize them!

What is most important to you? Is it important that you receive instant gratification or is it more important that you make investments that will provide benefits well in the future?

What Goals Do You Want to Accomplish?

As you look to focus on what is important for you, it is critical that you create specific and measurable goals. For example, if you want to get into shape, you may set specific milestones coupled with a plan to get there. Whatever you do, be intentional and set a timeline with measurable outcomes. If you want a new career, you may need to establish a timeframe for going back to school and updating your resume or creating a networking strategy.

Your goals should be in direct connection to the things that are important to you and your dreams for the future. One of my favorite quotes about goals comes from Greg Reid: "A dream written down with a date becomes a goal. A goal broken down into steps becomes a plan. A plan backed by action makes your dreams come true." What are you waiting for? Start working on your goals and plans today!

Stop Doubting and Start Believing

Recently, I was talking to a friend. She said: "Carlos, you are so confident, and I admire the videos and inspirational messages you share!" She went on to say that she is not confident. Like my friend, we all have negative experiences that erode our confidence. We need to get to the source of our insecurity and come to the realization that insecurity is not a place where we must stay.

I too have lacked confidence to do certain things, but I have learned to move in faith despite my fears or lack of confidence. Amazing things have happened in the process! We must unlearn the lies that we are not good enough or smart enough. Oftentimes our value has been misappropriated by others and the time is now to take back the value stolen from us!

Here is a little secret: When you start thinking more positive thoughts about yourself, you will be more confident to take risks and do things that you thought you could not do. And when you step out on faith and start having success, you will become more confident! The next time you start thinking negative thoughts about yourself, tell yourself to shut up! Then tell yourself: "Impossible is possible for me, there are no limits to what I can do."

Start believing that you can accomplish your goals and dreams even before you have a plan. That confidence will better position you to create and execute one. Quit putting others' needs before yours all the time and focusing on pleasing people at the expense of what is important to you!

The time is now to vote for you! Quit doubting yourself and letting others count you out! It's time to believe in you! If you don't believe in yourself, who else will? It's time to get your name on the ballot and cast your vote for "You!" Because YOU are worth it!

Parting Thoughts on Voting for YOU

I want you to start thinking of a candidate who has the capacity to do anything they set their mind to do. A candidate who is intelligent, fierce, handsome, beautiful, confident, and unstoppable! That candidate is you! The time is now to "vote for you!" Stop doubting yourself and comparing yourself to others. Stop speaking negative thoughts that impair your ability to walk in your passion and purpose! Focus on what is important and set meaningful and measurable goals.

FOR REFLECTION
"Stop doubting and start believing!"
~Carlos T. Carter

- What are some things holding you back from voting for yourself?
- What actions can you take to overcome barriers to voting for yourself?
- What are key goals and dreams you want to accomplish?
- What can you do today to start accomplishing your goals?

13 – DIFFERENT IS DOPE!
What Makes You Different Makes You Great!

In April 2019, I was the keynote speaker for a Celebration of US event at North Allegheny School District. They wanted me to talk about valuing differences, and I came up with this theme: Your Difference is Dope! The event was well planned and organized by the Community Diversity Group (I was part of the group). It was a great event with impressive performance by many minority groups in the district.

Although I thoroughly enjoyed the event, I was disappointed very few of the predominantly white residents of the district attended. I was disappointed, because I believed that the majority in the district needed to see the talents and beauty of many of the marginalized communities and ethnic groups that participated and, of course, I would have loved for them to hear my presentation. Especially given that many of the minority students often felt like they did not fit in. It could have been a great opportunity to spread knowledge, awareness, and understanding of different cultures and expressions.

I truly believe that to be great, you must value not only your differences, but also other people's. The current level of intolerance in the world is alarming, unacceptable, and not conducive to everyone being their authentic selves, realizing their potential, and living their best lives.

Being different is dope. The things that make you different make you special like color of your skin, your personality, your talents, or your quirky ways. We live in a world that is comprised of 7.53 billion people. According to the U.S. Census in 2018, only about 32.7 million live in the United States. That is a big number and could make one individual appear small or insignificant. Everyone is unique and has a potential to bring beauty and dopeness to the world. How do you learn to appreciate your dopeness and the dopeness of others? That is a good question. I think I have a few answers!

How To Discover Your Dopeness

The first step to discovering your dopeness is understanding and taking inventory of what makes you special. You can do this by listening to good things your family or friends say about you and observing how people respond to you. Look at the things you are passionate about and the impact it has on yourself and others.

When I was growing up, I never really had this type of mindset and did not take inventory of what makes me special. Had you asked me that question five years ago, it would have been more difficult, but today I can say a few things that make me special:

- I have a positive attitude,
- I have an ability to inspire, motivate, and encourage others
- I have an ability to sing, write, speak, and bring goofy energy to most situations
- I have empathy and compassion for the underserved and marginalized
- I have a quirky sense of humor

I am certain you have things that make you special as well. When you take the time to enumerate them, it is not being conceited. The key is understanding your dopeness, and there is nothing wrong with that. After you take inventory of what makes you unique, don't be afraid to share it with others!

Discover the Dopeness of Others

The key to discovering the dopeness in others is to be curious. This often requires leaving your comfort zone. I love this quote from Dr. Michael Welp, founder of White Men as Full Diversity Partners, "Approach people with empathy and inquiry." I like this quote, because we are sometimes too quick to judge or shun others. We often put them in a box because of their differences. I believe a better approach is to be curious, observe and ask questions to get to know them. You may be surprised that the person who seems least like you may have something in common with you.

There was a lady in my exercise class who seemed like she was standoffish. I thought she was quiet and not much of a people person. A couple of times we were in the steam room after a workout and did not talk. One day I decided to leave my comfort zone and try to engage her in conversation. As I began to talk to her, I realized that she was very nice. Contrary to my preconceived notions, she had a great personality. I got to know her, and this lady is awesome. Now when I see her, we greet each other enthusiastically. We realized through conversation that we have a mutual friend. We all can be guilty of developing preconceived notions about people, but when we take the time to be curious, we will discover the dopeness of others and that is what diversity is all about.

Appreciate the Symphony

The final part of discovering the dopeness of others is learning to appreciate the symphony of diversity. Get to know people who are different from you; appreciate and celebrate what makes them different. Find opportunities for them to leverage their cultural experiences and knowledge. Ask their opinion and input for new ideas and diverse perspectives. Invite them to lunch, find opportunities to connect, and make them feel part of your group.

It is one thing to say you value differences and diversity, but it takes it to a whole new level when you facilitate inclusivity. I love this quote: "Diversity is inviting them to the party, but inclusion is inviting them to dance!" When someone is part of the symphony, they can bring their unique instrument. The blending of these diverse instruments is what makes the symphony special!

FOR REFLECTION
"After you take inventory of what makes you unique, don't be afraid to share it with others!"
~Carlos T. Carter

- What can you do today to appreciate your uniqueness and the uniqueness of others?
- Do you have any preconceived notions about people or groups you don't know?
- What can you do to create a more inclusive environment at your job and in your community?

14 – BELIEVE IN CHANGE
Breaking Free from the Past

There have been times in my life where I struggled to forgive myself for my past mistakes. I would reflect on mistakes I made as a young father, and I would harbor those things in my mind. I even struggled from the shame of being an abuse survivor. I had to recognize that those were things that I did not have control over and had to push forward step by step, day by day.

I have learned to embrace the present and promise of the future. Unfortunately, there are some who are not able to move on from the pain, mistakes, and regrets of the past or people who constantly remind them of their mistakes. For some who can move forward, there are always those who will try to hold things over their head. How does one move from the past to embrace the present and promise of the future?

Forgive Yourself

One of the hardest things to do is to forgive yourself. Beating yourself up for past mistakes does not generate anything positive. There is nothing you can do to change the past, but you can have an impact on how you approach the future. Often the same harshness that you use on yourself reflects what was projected by your parents or others.

A good example is that you could have grown up in a home where your parents were strict or had very high expectations for you. If you did not make the expected grades or performed below their expectations, you may have experienced criticism. This experience may cause you to be hard on yourself. As a young father, I was sometimes strict or demanding of my kids. I now believe that part of it came from my own experiences growing up. As a result, it caused a few of my kids to be overly hard on themselves. I had to ask for forgiveness from them.

Despite many forces that can contribute to your inability to forgive yourself, you need to understand that you are not perfect. Although you may be committed to excellence and doing the best that you can, provide space for your humanity and imperfection. This understanding allows you to move from the past into the future.

Break Free from What Others Think

In 2020, I wrote a blog post about how I gained my freedom. I talked about how in my teens and early 20s, I struggled with worrying about what other people thought about me. I talked about how I signed up for a leadership coach and as we became more acquainted we discussed various subjects that were on my mind. She later commented on how open I was during our initial conversation. I explained to her that was not always the case for me. I added that being open with my feelings was not the culture that I grew up in. She asked me how I gained my freedom; I replied, "I desperately wanted my freedom." I used to criticize myself for various reasons, but when I truly learned to accept myself for who I am and not worry about what others thought about me, I became free.

I did not overthink her question. I simply told her that I wanted to be free to live authentically; free to be me without the weight of worrying about what others thought of me, and free to be who I am without being perfect. In fact, after I realized that perfectionism is a trap, I felt free.

No matter who you are and where you are in life, you should fight for your freedom. Freeing yourself from perfectionism and the opinions of others takes courage. Nevertheless, it will give you a level of power and joy that is unmatched.

By freedom, I am not saying you should not be ethically and morally accountable for your behavior, but you should be free to know and accept who you are and live your truth. Someone once said, "When you know who you are, you become empowered, but when you accept who you are, you become invincible!"

When you realize that other people's opinions are not important and do not define who you are, that puts you in the position to gain your freedom and break free from what others think about you. Getting to this place of freedom is not easy, but it is worth it.

Embrace God's Grace

I talked about forgiving yourself. But as a Christian, I feel like I get extra assistance from grace, because God has provided it to anyone who believes in him through his death and resurrection. God is a forgiving God. If I repent and ask for his forgiveness all is forgiven. In I John 1:9, it says, "If we confess our sins, he is faithful and just to forgive our sins and to cleanse us from all unrighteousness. (KJV)"

That does not mean that I have a pass to live recklessly, but that we have a God who is forgiving. Therefore, you may ask God for forgiveness as your process for moving forward from the past to embracing the future. Having this additional level of grace will position you for greater freedom to move forward from the past and to embrace a bright future.

We talked about forgiving ourselves, freeing ourselves from what others may think, and embracing God's grace. We also must believe that change can occur. We can all agree that moving from the past into the future is important to embrace the greatness that is within us. But none of that matters if you do not believe that change is possible. You can move forward from the past to embrace the promise and hope for the future. Believe that change is possible for you and for others.

Lack of forgiveness and believing in the possibility of change in our society is rampant. I look at how people look at others who have committed a crime and paid their debt to society; a lot of people still look down on them and won't give them a second chance, which is reflective of the state of the hearts of many. Unfortunately, this lack of forgiveness we refuse to give to others who have committed crimes and paid their debt is the same lack of forgiveness and lack of belief in people's ability to change which we apply to ourselves sometimes.

Believe in change. Disbelief in change is damning; and it condemns.

If we believe in seasons changing, why can't we believe in people changing? The world will become a better place for all when we believe in the power of forgiveness and change. After all, we all need second chances. You deserve a second chance as well as others. I challenge you today to believe in change for all. This belief will empower you and others to embrace the hope of the present and future and discover the greatness that awaits you. The opposite is true as well, when you don't believe in change, the future looks a lot bleaker for you and others.

FOR REFLECTION
"Believe in change. Know that your best days are not behind you, but ahead!"
~Carlos T. Carter

- What are some things from the past that hold you back from embracing the promise of the present and future?
- What can you do differently to believe in change for yourself and others?

"New beginnings are often disguised as painful endings."
~Lao Tzu

15 – NO SHORTCUTS, PLEASE!
There is No Easy Way to Achieve Success

In the fall 2018, my youngest son Isaiah and I were headed to Geneva College in Beaver Falls, PA to watch high school playoff games. I do not remember which teams were playing, but we were excited to watch some good basketball and meet up with friends and family.

After we parked the car, we hurried to the complex to get to the game. As we approached, we saw that there were several options to get to the gym. Keep in mind, this was a usually rainy season in Pittsburgh and there were mudslides at the time. I did not think of that before I decided to take a shortcut. The only thing on my mind was to get to this game as soon as possible and get a good seat. Isaiah made it down the hill just fine. I went next and started going down at a good pace. Suddenly I started to slide and lost my footing. I landed on my backside and went quickly down the hill. I looked like an emaciated pig who had been playing in the mud. People saw me and laughed. My son wanted to laugh, but was concerned and instead, asked: "Dad, are you okay?"

I was okay, for the most part. The biggest bruise was to my ego. I was muddy, wet, and embarrassed. I told my son to go in without me and I had his uncle give him a ride home. I learned later from my wife that my son was laughing to himself, but I believe he contained it to preserve his father's dignity!

Yes, this story is hilarious, but the truth is that we all can be guilty of taking shortcuts. Can you think of a time in your life when you wanted to achieve something and tried to find the easiest way? I'm sure you have. I'm not against efficiency, but there are no shortcuts to success! Success is a process and doesn't come before work. The only place where "success" comes before "work" is in the dictionary.

Put in the Work

Anything worth having requires work. We look at successful professional athletes, businesspeople, actors, and other professionals and are awed by their talent. However, the average person spends at least 10,000 hours to become an expert.

I love the popular meme on the internet that shows an iceberg sticking out of the water with the word "success" written on it. Beneath the surface are the words: persistence, failure, sacrifice, disappointment, dedication, hard work, good habits. Here is a funny thing about success: when it comes to the surface, it looks pretty on the outside, but people don't see what it took to achieve that success.

No matter what you want to achieve in life, you must be willing to put in your work. I am tired now as I write this chapter but am pushing through because I believe it is important to share my message of hope and encouragement. I believe that everyone has greatness inside, and I want to do my part to help encourage and unlock that greatness. I want all people to realize their full potential and live their best lives. You must be willing to put in the heart work and hard work. By heart work, I mean putting your heart and soul, and blood and sweat into pursuing your dreams. When you are passionate about what you are looking to accomplish it makes it a lot easier.

Unfortunately, there are folks who want success and just sit back and complain and procrastinate. Instead of doing that, admit that you are not willing to do what it takes to achieve your aspirations! You've got to want it. Go beyond wishful thinking and hoping. Create a plan and keep pushing, working, and believing until you achieve what is most important to you! Your dreams don't work unless you do!

Be Patient

I am not credentialed to write this section about patience. I am a strong Type A personality who wants things done yesterday. However, I have the wisdom to know that the race is not given to the swift. I know that patience is important for the race that requires endurance.

In September 2014, I ran in the Uphill 5K race, which is essentially a race where you run up a very steep Hill (Centre Avenue) in the historic Hill District. As I started the race, there was a guy with dreads and red shorts who just took off and passed me up. I thought, "Wow. I cannot keep up with this guy!" I said that I am going to go at a steady pace, because these hills are steep, and I will accelerate when it makes sense. As I proceeded up the Hill and eventually looked back, I realized that I had passed up the guy with the dreads! I was shocked as he started off fast but seemed to have quickly lost steam. There is a lesson here. As you climb the hill of success, be patient. Be measured as you pursue your goals, because you might run out of steam if you are impatient and move too fast.

No matter how badly you want your success, be patient as it does not happen overnight. There will be ups and downs, setbacks, failures, challenges, and triumphs, but you must be patient and steady to win the race.

Trust The Process

Success is not a destination but a journey. It is a process with many twists and turns. When you land in a destination that you perceive as success, there are always challenges. I remember when I served as a portfolio manager at Fifth Third Bank for 5 years and transitioned to my dream role as senior vice president and relationship manager at Bank of America. I was elated. This was a new role where I would lead business banking initiatives in the Pittsburgh region. It was a very competitive process, but I was able to prevail in the interview process through much hard work, determination, and prayer. And quite frankly, I was excited to be in a new and healthier work environment.

I faced many challenges in this new role working to build a new market from scratch. It was no easy task to bridge the investment side to the banking side to grow relationships. There were cultural barriers that were out of my control. Although I had reached what I perceived as my success destination, it was just part of my journey. I had many hurdles, good times, and disappointments during this assignment. But it challenged me to move out of my comfort zone and to become more comfortable with being uncomfortable. It taught me how to better navigate different people and situations, and to work in environments where there weren't many who looked like me or who could connect with my culture. It gave me high visibility opportunities with the market and media and helped me hone my presence and public speaking skills. Although this specific success journey ran its course after a few years, it gave me great confidence in who I am and what I am made of as a person. It positioned me for current success as a nonprofit leader, motivational speaker, and writer.

Although I thought this opportunity was a final success destination, it was just the beginning of a journey connecting me to my passion and purpose. My success journey continues. Each day writes a page that culminates into a chapter contributing to the book of my life story and journey. Enjoy the journey, what looks like success today, may look differently tomorrow. It is through the process that your impurities are burned off and character is created.

As you embark on your success journey, quit trying to take shortcuts and rush success. Respect the process and journey!

FOR REFLECTION
"No matter what you want to achieve in life, you must be willing to put in your work."
~Carlos T. Carter

- What are the most important goals you'd like to accomplish at this point in your life?
- What is standing in the way of success for you? What can you do about it?
- What does success look like for you?
- What can you do to create more success in your life?

16 – GET OUT OF YOUR COMFORT ZONE
Learn to be Comfortable with Being Uncomfortable

When you leave your comfort zone and face your fears, there is no limit to what you can accomplish! In early 2020, I booked an Airbnb for the first time to get away for a few days to work on my book and another project. The Airbnb was in a busy section of Oakland in Pittsburgh where many college students and other professionals live. Ideally, I wanted to leave the state, but given the weather and price this was the best option for me, or so I thought.

I was excited to go on my first writing retreat and made sure that I had a place with a fully equipped kitchen to allow me to prepare my own meals and focus on getting some writing done. On the day of my trip, I looked more closely at my reservation and started to realize that I may not be the only one in the apartment. The thought of it did not sit well with me and made me feel anxious. I had my own room, but I had no desire to be in a small apartment with a stranger. It was a totally foreign concept to me that I was willing to pass up.

Next, I reached out to the host and my worst fear was confirmed. She told me that I had only rented a room and would be in fact sharing the space. The prospect of being in a small apartment with a stranger was disconcerting and I was ready to cancel my reservation and forfeit my money.

Even though I was packed and ready to go, I had to take a couple pregnant mental pauses.
I absolutely did not want to be with a stranger, but at the same time, I knew how important it was to complete my book. As I paused, I said to myself, "If you want to complete your book, you have to be willing to leave your comfort zone!" I said to myself: "If this does not work out, I will return home!"

When I arrived, I could not get into the building. I was not able to figure out how the system worked and wondered if this was a bad omen. Eventually, I called the host and she helped me figure it out. Upon entering the unit, I was pleased to find it clean and cozy. However, the first thing that caught my attention was a dirty pair of Reeboks at the front door. They gave me the impression that someone had been walking in mud. I paused and wondered who was in this apartment, but the roommate was nowhere to be found and the extra bedroom door was closed. I thought this person may be creepy just based on the sight of those shoes.

I unpacked and did some writing in the kitchen most of the day and then locked my bedroom door to turn in around 9 p.m. As I was watching TV, I heard someone enter the apartment. I was thinking, "The stranger has now entered the apartment." I did not open my door to greet the person and I was not enthusiastic about it.

The next morning, I reluctantly opened the door and there was the roommate. He was a slim young man in his early twenties. He was wearing shorts with no shirt or shoes. He had arrived from Austria a couple weeks earlier to attend Carnegie Mellon University. We talked briefly as he was getting ready for class, but he was upbeat and pleasant. We had breakfast together my last day and I learned a lot about Austria and a few other things!

After meeting him, I was at ease. Ironically, I was uncomfortable sharing the apartment with a stranger, but he was gone most of the time and I got a lot of writing done. This experience reinforced the value of challenging myself to step outside my comfort zone. Although I always encourage others to leave their comfort zones, this experience reminded me that I have work to do. I would bet there are areas in your life where you need to stretch and challenge yourself as well. Leave your comfort zone.

Quit Playing It Safe

I once heard someone say, "If you do what you've always done, you will get what you've always gotten!" That is one of the major risks of playing it safe. You miss out on many good opportunities. Just like in basketball, if you do not take any shots because you are afraid, you will never have an opportunity to actually make a shot.

While I can be a risk taker at times, my natural inclination is to stay in between the lines. Recently, I was reading *Spiritual Leadership* by J. Oswald Sanders, and there was a part that caught my attention: "More failure comes from excess use of caution than from bold experiments with new ideas." I found this statement to be enlightening and true.

It made me think of how I let fear reign earlier in my life. I am blessed that I have learned the importance of stretching myself even when I am afraid. I have learned to just do it, focusing more on the opportunity than the possibility of failure. This perspective has given me the courage to be a motivational speaker, leader, and better person. After all, according to Nelson Mandela, "Courage is not the absence of fear, but the triumph over it." I will talk more about facing fears in principle number eighteen.

Become Comfortable with Being Uncomfortable

When I worked for a bank, I ran into a successful female financial advisor. She was one of the few Black female financial advisors in in the Pittsburgh region. She had to face many challenges climbing to her current level as a Black woman in a male-dominated field. She worked hard to create the success she currently enjoys, and I remember her saying on many occasions that she had to learn to become comfortable with being uncomfortable.

Like my coworker, I too had to learn to become comfortable with being uncomfortable because I have often been the only Black person or only Black male working in a predominately white male-dominated banking industry. I had to learn to become comfortable with being uncomfortable. I would go to bank meetings and other networking events and would be the only one. This was never easy, but I was determined to be successful; networking and building relationships was critical to that goal. I pushed past my comfort zone because there were things I wanted to accomplish.

Always Be Open to Change

Anything that is not growing is dying. If you are stuck in your ways you will not go far in life. I've been around people who are set in their ways, and I have witnessed their stagnation. Many of these people also stagnate others. When you are open to change, you will find opportunities for growth and to leave your comfort zone. If you are successful but remain static, your days are numbered because you will find yourself irrelevant. The typewriter was replaced by the computer and the CD was replaced by digital music. If you are willing to: quit playing it safe, become comfortable with being uncomfortable, and always be open to change, you will truly position yourself to do great things!

FOR REFLECTION
"Anything that is not growing is dying."
~Carlos T. Carter

- What are areas of your life where you have become too complacent?
- What is keeping you from leaving your comfort zone?
- What is the one area that you could make the greatest impact by leaving your comfort zone?

17 – Don't Sweat It
Calm in the Middle of the Storm

As a nonprofit executive, father, husband, motivational speaker, blogger, former banker, and anything else you want to add (hopefully all good), I know that life can be good and stressful. There are times when I am as cool as a cucumber and other times when I am sweating like a pig!

I am certain that you can relate to my experiences. You may have a lot going on and I understand that it can be hard to remain focused. You may also have many demands on your time. Juggling multiple priorities can be stressful. If you are a taskmaster like me, you are always thinking of things that need done. And God bless all the mothers because they really have a lot on their plates trying to manage families and careers. If you are a stay-at-home parent, you have a huge job managing your family corporation!

I have done my share of worrying, but it has only led to stress and anxiety over things that I cannot control. I have worried about not having enough money to pay my bills when I had job losses. I have worried about my kids staying focused, getting good grades, and hanging out with the wrong crowds and peer pressure. I have worried, as I prepared for board meetings, about not knowing how certain board members would respond to current situations or proposals.

Finally, I was especially worried during the COVID-19 pandemic that took many lives and caused financial devastation to people and economies around the world. During the pandemic, I had to constantly keep myself and others focused to handle the many concerns related to that very serious situation.

Although we cannot control the vicissitudes of life, we can change how we respond to them. You may be asking yourself, how can I have more peace, despite all the things going on around me? It is a myth that to have peace, everything must be calm as you sip tea or a margarita and listen to birds chirping while soaking up the sun on a beach.

Peace doesn't mean the absence of challenges, trouble, or controversy. Peace is the ability to be calm despite everything around you. Peace is focusing on what you can control instead of what you cannot. This sentiment is something that I continue to discover as I navigate this thing called life. Having peace in the middle of the storm puts you in a better place mentally and physically, as we know stress can have adverse effects on the mind, body, and soul.

Stress can cause aches, pains, insomnia, stomach problems, lack of clear thinking, weakening of your immune system, weight fluctuations, depression and more.

Focus On What You Can Control

All you can do is all you can do! A father who was a new coach met the venerable Coach John Wooden and asked for his advice about coaching his son's young team. John told him, "Don't worry about beating the other team but focus on what you can control!" That is important as we try to control things that we cannot and get ourselves all stressed out over things that are bigger than us. If we simply focus on what we can control, we will have more peace and get more accomplished. Don't worry about what you cannot control.

This lesson is easier repeated than executed but can make a difference in your peace and happiness. I constantly must remind myself that I cannot control everything and that is okay. During the COVID-19 pandemic, I was overwhelmed because I was often fearful of my kids and others bringing germs into the house and that simply drove me crazy. I had to get to a point where I accepted that all I can do is take basic precautions, as I cannot control the actions of others. I was often fearful about tough decisions that I may need to make at work to keep the nonprofit I worked for viable, and I had to simply remind myself to focus on what I can control. This decision has enabled me to sleep much better at night.

Live Life in Day-Tight Compartments

A great principle lived by the late, great Dale Carnegie was coined by Sir William Osler. Osler came across a quote from Thomas Carlisle which said, "It is our goal to see what lies dimly in the distance but to do what clearly lies at hand."

I first discovered this concept while reading Dale Carnegie's *How to Stop Worrying and Start Living.* In this book, he talks about not focusing on the past and not thinking too far in the future but living life in 24-hour compartments. Adopting this philosophy helps you focus and do what you can do within a 24-hour block versus becoming overwhelmed by the past or what is ahead. This principle is great for living a peaceful life. I suggest you give it a try.

I personally struggle with staying in the present given my thinker and planner personality. The challenge with that is that you can get bogged down by things in the future and your ability to live in and focus on the present will be stymied. This is especially challenging for Type A personalities who are more challenged with relaxing. My wife is Type B and has no problem living in the present and just relaxing (I truly envy her for that natural inclination). Even though something is not your natural inclination, it does not mean that you cannot work toward being more chill and living within the day. You can do it, my friend!

Believe In Something Bigger Than Yourself

As a Christian, I rely on my faith (as discussed in Chapter 4). My faith is important to me, and it helps immensely with stress. I have learned to pray and put my concerns in God's hands and trust that he will work them out. Wow, this principle is a major burden lifter for me! You must find what works for you. I strongly believe having faith in a higher power is a game changer and it can give you peace which goes beyond logic or understanding!

Looking back at the many challenges I have discussed in the earlier chapters of this book; I do not know how I would have made it without faith. Don't get me wrong there were times when my faith has been questioned and challenged. During my second job loss, I did not have much faith at all and thought everything was pretty much over for me. I was in deep dark despair. But when I regained my faith, it gave me such peace and enabled me to rest knowing that everything would work out for me and that there is a higher power that loves and cares for me and wants me to win. One of my favorite scriptures is Jeremiah 29:11, "For I know the plans I have for you, declares the Lord, plans to prosper and not to harm you, plans to give you hope and future (NIV)." This is one of my scriptures that I like to reflect upon in hard times. Through my faith, I know that I do not have to worry because God will take care of me. Just the thought of that puts me at ease.

Find An Outlet

Whether it's painting, dancing, building model planes, hiking, or engaging in another activity, it is important to have things that take you away from stress and put you in a place of peace. For some, it may be yoga; for me, it is exercising. I love to exercise. The mental and physiological effects are wonderful. Exercising is my drug of choice. It truly helps me to free my body from the cortisol or stress hormones.

One day I was working from home and was very stressed. I had seven Zoom meetings and was Zoomed-out. I could feel how tense my neck and body were. I mentioned to my wife about how I was feeling, and she said, "Carlos, is it probably from the stress you have been under lately?" After our conversation, I went for a short run around my neighborhood. I had the bonus of running into neighbors who were having a block party with music, and I had the opportunity to dance before I finished up my run. After the running and dancing, I was totally relaxed. I felt free and my whole mood changed. If you have not discovered what works for you, you need to explore until you find it!

Take A Breath

There is nothing more refreshing than taking a deep breath when you are feeling stressed. Unfortunately, when you are feeling anxious, you tend to breathe more shallowly from the chest. Learning to take deep breaths through the nose that fill the abdomen can provide much needed relief. This breathing technique reduces the stress hormone Cortisol and provides a healthy dose of oxygen to the brain. It puts you more at ease and provides greater clarity of thought. Further, it slows down the heart rate and takes you out of the fight or flight mode. It establishes greater peace and harmony within your body.

I am no mindfulness expert, but during my Lead Now Pittsburgh leadership training (prestigious 12-month leadership fellowship through Leadership Pittsburgh) that is the first thing they taught us: to be more mindful and focused through deep breathing. I do this often when I am stressed and need to relax my mind for greater clarity and focus. It is a good technique when someone says something you don't like or that is triggering or causes you to lose your focus. For example, one day, I was at a meeting and a guy made statements that upset me. Instead of reacting openly, I intentionally dropped my pen under the table and took a deep slow breath to get myself together. When I sat up in my seat, I refrained from saying anything that I may have regretted.

Manage Those Thoughts

In the first chapter *"About those Thoughts!"* I talked about the importance of managing your thoughts and suggested things to help you manage them. When you have negative or worrisome thoughts, have positive affirmations to replace them. If you worry a lot about bad things happening, you need to learn to speak life to those situations and have positive thoughts. Instead of saying, "I am going to fail at this," say, "I can do this. I am strong and capable." For me, I would say," I can do all things through Christ who strengthens me!" You must find what works for you. But the point is that your thoughts are a big part of worrying. If you focus more on the positive and not the negative, you will have a lot less to worry about.

Why are you stressing and sweating? Start focusing on what you can control. Start living in day-tight compartments and leverage these recommendations for having more peace and less stress in your life. Life is too short to be pressed and stressed! Embrace the peace that is waiting for you!

FOR REFLECTION
"All you can do is all you can do!"
~Carlos T. Carter

- What are the things that make you worry?
- Come up with positive affirmations to counter each worry-filled thought listed above.

18 – Face Your Fears
Courage to Overcome

In chapter 16, I talked about getting out of your comfort zone, but in this chapter, I want to talk more about the root of fear and how we can overcome it.

As I proceeded to write, I already had my own observations and experiences with fear. I decided to pause and turn to the all-knowing Google out of curiosity. I Googled: "What causes fear?" and was taken to a page written by Dr. Paul Ekman who says: "The universal trigger for fear is the threat of harm, real or imagined. This threat can be for our physical, emotional, or psychological well-being. While there are certain things that trigger fear in most of us, we can learn to become afraid of nearly anything."

Although fear can be healthy and protect us from danger (such as being hit by a car, avoiding a falling object, or anything else to protect our physical or emotional wellbeing), it can cripple us and stop us from living fully. For example, let's take a strategy of avoiding people who harm us emotionally. There are people whom I have avoided because they are triggers for me. I had a colleague who was negative, abrasive, and confrontational. I tried to avoid her like the plague. There was a man who was toxic and rude whom I avoided as well. Fear is an issue when it stops you from living fully or deeply. This persistent fear and anxiety challenge your ability to live, cope, and manage. As I mentioned in prior chapters, I was depressed and anxious after a job loss. I feared losing my house and, not finding a job. My fear was paralyzing. I was immobilized by it until I met with a therapist who helped me to realize that my fears were not going to come true. If I am honest, that was not the first time that I was ruled by fear. I grew up in an environment where fear was dominant.

My mother went through many challenges during her childhood that caused a lot of fear in her life. I believe that fear was transferred to my siblings and me in similar ways. Things like being cautious of people and being more secretive and less open to share real emotions and feelings. It perpetuated operating on the surface because of fear of being hurt. It limited our ability to be vulnerable and trust others with our hearts. When you have these emotional fears and traumas, they preclude you from having deeper relationships and connections that can help you to have strong and healthy relationships. If you allow it, it will limit your ability to live fully. I believed that the world is a dangerous place, and I needed to be cautious. This fear was further reinforced by the subsequent childhood traumas of abuse that I discussed earlier in this book. I am proud to say that I continue to grow and persevere daily and have gained my freedom from this mindset.

We know that everybody has fears, and you and I are not alone. Some choose to move ahead despite their fears, while others are paralyzed and imprisoned. If you are ruled by fear, you are not living! You know prison isn't just a place, but a state of mind. I was in prison until I learned to break free. I will talk more about this shortly. You may appear free to others on the outside, while internally you are caged by fear. Facing and overcoming your fears is the key that unlocks your prison doors and the greatness that is within. It frees you to walk into the opportunities that come with having the courage to pursue your passion and purpose. It empowers you to be free and all that God has created you to be!

I remember when my fears drove my decisions and limited my possibilities. I did not go out for sports in high school because I was afraid of failing. I signed up for track and cross county but did not follow through. I pushed people away because I did not know if they would like me. These things were based on fears that, by the grace of God, I have learned to overcome. I am glad to be in the position to share strategies to help you, or to help you help someone who is dealing with the bondage of fear.

When I think about my motivational blogs and videos, I freely share my personal thoughts and feelings to motivate and empower others to discover their greatness. Someone commented on my confidence, "Carlos, you are so confident to do the things that you do." I would have never done that in my twenties or thirties.

When I was in a dark place, depressed and overwhelmed with fear, my good friend Jason J. Washington recommended I see a Christian counselor named Sam. I connected with a nice gentleman, probably in his forties. I admit that the thought of meeting him made me fearful and unsure, but he was kind and compassionate. I knew that If I wanted to change my life and pull myself out of my rut that I needed someone to help me. The counselor was easy to talk and relate to, and I connected with him quickly. He was empathetic and had similar traumatic corporate working experiences. I genuinely treasured our time together. We even had joint sessions that included my wife. I credit him with helping me get to the place that I am today.

A key lesson Sam taught me about fear is that fear does not mean that whatever you fear will come true. During one session, he asked me to write down my fears which was an interesting exercise. No one had ever asked me about my fears, let alone asked me to make and keep a list of them. I remember reflecting on that list a year after my sessions ended, and I realized that none of them came true! This makes me wonder why I wasted time on things that did not come true. I learned from that experience to never let fear rule my life or dictate my decisions.

The late great motivational speaker Zig Ziglar defines fear as "False Expectations Appearing Real." I love his definition of fear as it speaks to the fact that many fears are irrational. We often worry about things that we cannot control or things that simply will not come true. You may be asking yourself what can I do to overcome fear? Well, I'm glad you asked!

Speak Life

In the first chapter, "About Those Thoughts!" and other chapters, I talked about the importance of controlling your thoughts. I cannot talk about this enough. Author Levi Lusko stated that the human brain has an average of 500 negative or intrusive thoughts within a sixteen-hour day, each lasting fourteen seconds. Those are a lot of negative thoughts. You must find a way to focus on the positive versus the negative. When negative or fearful thoughts come to mind, you must have positive thought quotes or phrases to counter them. One of my favorite scriptures is Philippians 4:8 which states: "Finally, brothers and sisters, whatever is true, whatever is noble, whatever is right, whatever is pure, whatever is lovely, whatever is admirable -- if anything is excellent or praiseworthy -- think about such things. (NIV)." This is the essence of speaking life.

Given that most of our thoughts are negative, we must corral these thoughts and replace them with the positive. At times, when you tell yourself that you cannot do something or you think of negative outcomes to situations, replace that thinking with positive thoughts. For example, if you are looking to start a business, don't let fear overtake you by saying, "It will never work!" or "People won't be interested in my product or service!" Instead say, "I have done my research and believe this will work!" The next time you are fearful to do anything new, change the narrative from, "This won't work!" to "I got this!" Always talk and focus more on why you should, instead of why you shouldn't. Stop doubting yourself and speaking negative and destructive thoughts! Focus more on the possibilities and opportunities that lie ahead. There will always be things that can go wrong, but that should not be your focus!

Operate Despite Fear

People have complimented me and deemed me confident, since I am willing to share my thoughts and messages on video and write and share personal things. Yes, generally I am confident, but I have insecurities and fears just like everyone else. The difference is that I continue to learn to operate despite my fears. When I did my first video, I was very self-conscious and did not know if people would ridicule me. My passion to empower people to discover their greatness is more powerful than my fears or insecurities. There are times when I create a post and am afraid to share it for being too vulnerable or face negative comments or rejection, but I share it anyway.

Fear is just a feeling! Remember Nelson Mandela's words: "Courage is not the absence of fear, but the triumph over it!" We assume that people who have done great things are not afraid and that is simply not true they move despite fear. Learn to replace our fear with faith and allow your passion to be greater than your fear.

I have made the decision to have courage and have faith that things will work out despite my fears or insecurities. I am a witness that you'll become bolder and stronger when you push past your fear When you realize that you won't die if people criticize you or if you fail, you will be liberated! You must keep focused on what you are trying to accomplish and operate despite your fears. Let's face it: if your fears are dictating everything in your life, you are in prison. I refuse to let my fears stop me from fulfilling my passion and purpose and realizing the greatness that is within! Is it easy operating despite your fear? No! Is it worth it? Absolutely!

Remember Failure Is Not Fatal

Many people have a fear of failure that stops them from doing many things. I personally have been guilty of this but have come to realize that it is not the end of the world. When I lost my job and went into depression, I really thought things were over for me. I had a friend at the YMCA say to me, "Carlos, how many times can you reinvent yourself?"

Although he did not mean any harm, that statement was devastating for me. I shared it with my wife, and she said, "It only takes one opportunity. God has the final say!" Boy, was she right! I eventually found many opportunities. Although I do not make the money that I used to make in the banking world, my bills are paid, I'm healthy and guess what? I am living my passion and purpose as a nonprofit leader, motivational speaker, and blogger. And guess what? The money will eventually come. My focus is not on money but making an impact in the world. Don't believe the lie that your failure will be fatal, because in most cases that is not true. You can rebound, you can reinvent yourself. You can recover! Control those thoughts and don't let anything stop you from doing what you were created to do. Failure is not fatal and quite frankly, it is overrated! Learn to push through the fear of failure. You can come back. Failing is usually not the end of the world but is often part of the process to success.

Think About the Life You Want

Based on the many traumas I faced growing up in the fear-based mindset, I was limited when it came to living my best life. When I was overly worried about what people thought about me and even dealing with the shame of the past, I was not living my best life. When I resolved not to worry about what others thought of me, I became empowered in all aspects of my life. I looked at myself in the mirror and said, "I want better. I must have better. God has a plan and purpose for my life, and I am going to realize it! I am not going to let others put me in a box. I am not going to let fear imprison me!" It is conversations like this that put me on the path to living my best life. You don't want to come to the end of the road and realize that you never really lived because of your fears! Life is too short to let fear cut short lives that are already too short. If you are constantly living in fear, you are not living-you are already dead! Resolve today to live! Don't let anyone or anything stop you from living and enjoying life. Most importantly, don't let anything or anyone stop you from living your passion and purpose and realizing the greatness that God has placed inside you!

Seek Help

The first four guiding principles to overcome fear are great, but sometimes you need help. Thank God for my many friends, including Jason J. Washington and counselor. It is okay to reach out for help. It shows strength and courage to take the step to reach out and say, "I need help!" Being overly prideful and not getting help when you need it is not wise. If fear and anxiety are filling your life, I strongly suggest that you find a professional to help you navigate the process.

When you make the decision to operate despite your fears, you will realize that failure is not fatal. Endeavor to live a life with no regrets. Face your fears and don't let anything stop you from going after what is important to you!

FOR REFLECTION
"Face your fears and don't let anything stop you from going after what is important to you!"
~Carlos T. Carter

- How has fear impacted your ability to live with passion and purpose?
- What is your biggest fear?
- Which of the recommendations outlined in this chapter can you put into practice to push past fear?

19 – STAY CONNECTED
The Power of Networking

When you think about networking, what comes to mind? Are comfortable with it? Does it make you anxious? Do you see it as a waste of time? Do you think of handing out business cards at an event? Does friending on Facebook or connecting with someone on LinkedIn, Instagram, or other social media platforms come to mind? All these things are part of networking. I would like to share how networking has impacted my life and how you can become more comfortable with it. Before I share how networking has impacted my life, let's see what my friend Google has to say about networking.

Here are the definitions that I found from www.lexico.com for networking:

- "The action or process of interacting with others to exchange information and develop professional or social contacts" or
- "The linking of computers to allow them to operate interactively."

Although the first definition explains the textbook meaning, the second applies to computer networks, but is relevant to people. This definition talks about linking and operating interactively which is integral to networking.

I am an extroverted introvert; networking has not been as much a challenge for me as for other people. Even so, it has not been easy. People who have interacted with me personally may be shocked to hear me use "introvert" to describe myself in any way.

Although I am generally extroverted, I recharge alone, enjoy spending time alone, and dislike big crowds. This is ironic because I have no problem speaking or singing on any platform in front of large crowds. I guess my passion just takes over! I can be comfortable in large crowds; however, I tend to step back. I remember I was at a leadership retreat with my cohort from Lead Now Pittsburgh (a year-long leadership training of up to twenty-five people) and one of the people from my cohort Dr. Diamonte Walker came up to me and pointed out that I am an extroverted introvert like her. She observed my pulling back from the crowd. I was stunned by her observation, but also enlightened. She had figured me out because she was the same way.

Maybe I'm just weird! On a serious note, this observation from Dr. Walker underscored the importance of understanding who you are and what environments or settings make you feel most comfortable. This understanding can be helpful and transformative for people who may feel something is wrong with them. It is important to understand what your extrovert or introvert proclivities are. As you network, take time to understand how you are wired and don't be afraid to leave your comfort zone. Just because you have a proclivity to a certain style does not mean that you cannot stretch yourself to achieve your networking goals.

My first experiences with networking probably started with my foray into the banking world. While I was working in the dietary department at Montefiore University Hospital (now UPMC Montefiore), I was connected to a mentoring program that I mentioned at the beginning of the book. Although I did not know a lot about networking at that time, I was informally engaging in networking. My mentor, Al Harris was the director of facilities for the hospital system at that time. I was connected to him through a manager who was impressed with a letter I wrote during a dispute. I had a conflict with my immediate supervisor and believed he was trying to write me up for an inaccurately perceived infraction. I did not agree with his decision and wrote a letter of appeal to his manager. The manager was so impressed that he referred me to a mentoring program in the hospital to try to get more minorities into leadership roles.

Initially, I was set up with another mentor and then connected with Mike. While in this program, I used to go to meetings with Mike and

I had the pleasure of listening in and watching how he conducted himself. I learned a lot from these interactions as I had never been exposed to business meetings before. Since I was a recent college graduate, I was hoping that he would assist me with a new job. Although I never remember asking him directly, I did let him know about my major and my aspirations. I hoped and prayed that he would try to help me. One day, while in his office, he said to me, "I like you! You would interview well. Give me your resume and I will share it with my wife who is head of Corporate Staffing at Mellon Bank (now BNY Mellon)."

Although I did not know a lot about networking at the time, I was in fact networking. I was building a relationship and making a connection with a person who led me to several job opportunities. You see, networking is all about building relationships. Some people only focus on handing out business cards or connecting online. You must keep in mind that people like doing business with people they know, and that trust is built through relationships. We will talk a little more about trust later.

My experience with Mike was one of many instances where networking played a key part in my life and led to job opportunities. Another that comes to mind is when I transitioned out of the banking world and was trying to land a job as an executive director of a nonprofit. As I mentioned in another chapter, it was a difficult transition for me from the banking world. I was trying to do something I was more passionate about. I wanted a job where I could better leverage my skills, talents, and leadership abilities.

One day while I was doing consulting for Nazareth Prep (part of Holy Family Institute), I went to an event at Manchester Bidwell Corporation. My goal was to increase my knowledge and make connections to help my job search. After the event, I made several new contacts and talked to my good friend Kevin Jenkins who was the chief operations officer of Manchester Bidwell at the time (now he is the CEO). He introduced me to a gentleman named Scott Lammie, then CFO of UPMC Health Plan, in Pittsburgh. I met Scott before at a fundraiser for the Boy Scouts, but I was not sure if he remembered me.

While Scott and I were talking, we started discussing people we knew in common, my background, and what I was looking to do. He said, "I know about an opportunity that you would be perfect for where you could leverage your business background as well." He went on telling me about an organization called Homeless Children's Education Fund (HCEF) and encouraged me to reach out to the current executive director Bill Wolfe (who was retiring soon) and tell him that I was referred by Scott.

I was excited for this lead, followed up with Bill by email the next day. I told him about Scott's referral. Bill sent my information to the headhunter who was managing the search for the next executive director. The rest is history. I was the executive director of HCEF for several years. I learned later that Scott Lammie was an important funder of the organization. He was recognized as a Champion for Children, an annual awards ceremony where HCEF recognizes local community champions who further the organization's mission to support children with their educational goals. Given Scott's connections and relationships, my referral from him received prompt attention. He has positively impacted many lives including mine. We have a special connection to this day, and I am forever grateful for this relationship!

There are so many ways networking has positively impacted my life – I could write a book on it. I would like to share principles to enable you to make and maintain key relationships to achieve your goals, dreams, and aspirations.

Six Keys To Successful Networking

1. Build Relationships – Many people see networking as only passing out and receiving business cards. Although business or contact information may be exchanged, networking is more about building relationships. If you approach things from the business card perspective, you will fail to network effectively. Ask open-ended questions like: "Tell me about yourself? Tell me more about X and Y? How can I help you with what you are working on?"

   A big part of networking is making a connection. Take the time to get to know the person. Try to understand their goals, dreams, and interests and don't be afraid to share the same about yourself. Finding out what you have in common will help you build a relationship and make a connection that goes beyond the superficial.

   Always remember that people like doing business with people they know and like. There is no better way to do this than making the time to sincerely get to know one other. When you seize the opportunity to build authentic relationships and make personal connections, people will go out of their way to help you achieve your goals and dreams.

2. Look to Help Others – Networking is a two-way street. It is more meaningful if each party benefits from the networking relationship. As you work to build your relationships and make connections with others, don't be shy about asking for help to achieve your goals and dreams. You should be equally passionate about offering your assistance to others. When you are genuinely willing to help others, you are planting seeds that will come back to you.

   I can remember a time when a close friend of mine, Kevion Latham, offered to help connect my son to a resource that would help him pay for school. I will never forget how he helped me in a time of great need. The main reason I believe he helped is because he is a good person who enjoys helping others. I also believe that he remembered how I helped him when he first started his career as a financial advisor. I knew that he was struggling to get clients, and I agreed to be his first client. He never forgot how I supported him back then. When you genuinely seek to help others, they will want to help you in return.

3. Get Out Of Your Comfort Zone – A key part of networking is your willingness to get out of your comfort zone. In Chapter 16 I discussed

getting out of your comfort zone more generally, but it is also critical to networking. If you are trying to do new things and meet new people, you must be willing to be uncomfortable and talk to people who may not look or think like you. When I was a banker in a predominately white male dominated field in Pittsburgh, I was always the only Black male at bank meetings and important business meetings.

It was very uncomfortable and awkward at times, and I had to really stretch and push myself to introduce myself to people and even politely crash group events to get to know people. Despite my discomfort, I met great contacts who have helped make key connections for me. No matter who you are, be willing to become comfortable with being uncomfortable. You must focus more on the opportunities that networking could bring and less on your fears. Keep in mind that most people are willing and want to be helpful! Challenging yourself will help you with invaluable connections to people with whom you can build great relationships, which will in turn help propel you forward to achieving your goals and dreams.

4. Take A Genuine Interest In Others – Having a genuine interest in others will always bode

well. Let's face it, most of us are self-centered and love when people listen, talk and care about what is important to us. I love this coaster that is in my house that says, "Let's talk more about how fabulous you think I am!" Every time I see that coaster, it puts a big smile on my face. Use this knowledge to invest in others. By taking a genuine interest in others, many will be more willing and concerned about helping you. Ask questions like:

- How did you get to where you are now?
- What can you tell me about your family?
- Why did you choose your current field?
- Who were the key people who helped make you the person you are today?

There are many things you can ask, and these are just a few sample questions. Whatever you do, be genuine. People can spot a phony a mile away. When you are genuine, you will set yourself apart. Superficial networkers will not be remembered.

5. Leverage Mentors and Sponsors – I cannot stress the importance of mentors and sponsors. Mentors are people who you look up to and who can give you guidance and a sense of direction. Sponsors are mentors who are willing to vouch for you on your

character, talent, and skills, and are willing to put their name on the line for you. They will say, "___ is a great person and you should interview them or meet with them." They are people who will go to bat for you to connect you to opportunities.

Make connections with potential mentors and sponsors. They will they help you grow personally and professionally, and help you make key connections to realize your potential and achieve your wildest dreams! I personally have benefitted from mentors and sponsors throughout my career and continue to benefit from their connections for key speaking and training opportunities.

6. Follow up – No matter how good you are with networking; you will never succeed if you don't follow up. When Scott Lammie mentioned the job opportunity at HCEF to me, I followed up immediately. Had I not followed up, I would not have had the opportunity to lead such a great organization for so many years. Use your calendar or other technology to remind you to follow up. Just imagine how many opportunities were missed because people did not follow up. Following up sets you apart from the competition.

People will see you as someone who takes initiative and keeps their word. Whether it is following up for a lunch or coffee meeting, a promised connection to help someone else, just to say thank you after someone has helped you, following up is always worthwhile. I have made a concerted effort to make sure that I thank people and remind them how they have helped me.

It is a myth that people can pull themselves up by their own bootstraps. You may work hard to achieve, but no one does anything great alone. A man named Curtis used to make me laugh when he would say, "Two heads are better than one as long as they are not on the same shoulders. If they were on the same shoulders, then you have a monster." When you connect with others you are working smarter instead of harder. Your willingness to do this creates limitless opportunities for you and those with whom you connect!

FOR REFLECTION
"No one is an island, and we all need others to help us get to where we want to be!"
~Carlos T. Carter

- What are your fears around networking?
- How can you become better at networking?
- What two principles above do you need to focus on at this point in your life?

20 – BELIEVE IN YOURSELF
Confidence is a Key Ingredient to Success

Recently, a nonprofit reached out for my help with coaching their team on how to gain more confidence. Additionally, a large school district approached me to help improve the confidence of their leaders I don't believe there is a PhD., or any degree, in confidence, and I don't have one. For each of these clients, I had to reflect deeply, and I had to research what makes people more confident. I had never thought about creating such a course for teaching people how to be more confident. As I reflect, I now realize that I have always encouraged people to believe in themselves. In my quest to empower others to follow their dreams, I was inadvertently teaching them to be more confident.

I can remember countless times when I would go to schools or talk to people one-on-one and help them see the value that they bring to the table. I remember specifically talking to a close friend of mine who is a leader and realized that he was insecure. I have worked with him to build his confidence.

In chapter (12) "Vote for You" I commented on the importance of self-confidence and how managing your thoughts is a big part of it. Yet, I did not develop some of the key components. In full disclosure, I was not going to do a chapter on self-confidence, but I had decided it was needed after listening to coach Darieth Chisolm discuss the importance of confidence for speakers who want to get paid in her video, *Speaking Fees for Authors.* As I listened, I thought to myself, *"Hmmm…if I am doing a book that helps people discover their greatness and become the best versions of themselves, how can they do that without confidence?"* What is confidence and how can you be more confident? I am glad you asked! Let's dive into it!

Let's start with the Carlos T. Carter definition of confidence:

> *"Confidence is the conviction that you are a valuable, capable, and competent to do anything if you work hard and make a good effort. Furthermore, you have trust in your capacity to accomplish goals and dreams. You believe you can add value in most situations."*

Now that you have the Carlos T. Carter definition of confidence, let's explore strategies to put it into action.

Positive Self-Talk

I know I covered this in the first chapter "About Those Thoughts," but we cannot talk about this enough. You are what you think and many of the thoughts that go through your mind are negative. According to Levi Lesko, as I have previously mentioned, people have an average of 500 intrusive thoughts in a 16-hour day – that is a lot! We must constantly fill our mind with positive thoughts.

When you have negative thoughts, you need to have positive affirmations to counter. For example, if you are thinking, "This is not going to work out." You need to replace it with, " I got this!" or "I am not ready for this interview; they are not going to like me!" to "Is this interview ready for me?" Or "I am not going to do this right… I always fail or mess up!" to "Everything will work out!" I talked about this in Chapter 18 - "Face Your Fears", as well! You must work every day to maintain positive self-talk.

If you find positive words and thoughts to counter the negative thoughts, you will be more confident and successful. More people will want to be around you because of your confidence and positive mindset.

Surround Yourself with Positive People

Have you ever been around people who were negative and always put you down? You may have experienced this in childhood or in adulthood. When I was working in one bank, there was a gentleman who appeared confident, but he was insecure and always put down others. He said negative things about me and others. This is not the type of energy that helped with confidence. I believe it is critical that we surround ourselves with positive people who are supportive, optimistic, and help bring out the best in us. When many of us struggle with self-esteem, the worst thing you could have around you is negative people who tear you down. Unfortunately, many of these people may be close to you like friends and family. However, to maintain or achieve positive self-esteem, you need to remove yourself from this toxicity, and limit your interactions with those people.

I can think of a particular relative in my family who is negative and toxic, but the individual seems to have no clue about the impact of their negativity on others. I have made the decision to limit contact with that person for my sanity. Although this individual does not necessarily impact my self-esteem, their energy is not conducive to anything positive, and I have had to remove myself from that energy as it is draining and demoralizing.

One of my favorite quotes from Joel Osteen says: "There should be people in your life that inspire you, that make you strive to do better. Eventually you're going to be like the people you are connected to." I would add that when you are around positive people, you will feel better about yourself. Whether you are trying to be more confident or want to maintain your confidence, hanging around positive people is good for the soul and spirit.

I can think of many friends like that, but one who comes to mind is Saleem Ghubril (author of my Foreword) who is the leader of the Pittsburgh Promise. He is an amazing and accomplished individual and leader. The key thing I like about him is that he makes everyone feel valued and important; he is very encouraging and uplifting. Anytime I have met with him as a mentor and friend he has always provided sound advice, but more importantly, he always uplifts your spirit and confidence. I am sure I have said it on many occasions that he is good for the soul! Saleem is a good example of the kind of person who helps us see the best in ourselves.

Practice and Experience

Practice and experience are an important part of confidence. The longer you live and can accomplish certain things and overcome obstacles, the more confident you will become in your abilities. There may be areas in your life where you are less confident, but that confidence will come with experience and practice. I can think of the time when my kids were learning to play basketball and could not dribble or shoot well. With practice and coaching, they became better. I remember when my middle son, Daylon, who is very competitive would cry when I would beat him in basketball (I'm not that good), and I kept telling him that one day he would be better than me.

Well, that came true very quickly in his preteen years, but he never would have gotten better without practice. I challenge you to identify areas where you may not be as confident and pursue the experience, practice, and coaching or mentorship you need to help get you to the next level. Don't be too hard on yourself if you are not confident in certain areas yet, you may just need more experience!

Eat The Meat, Spit Out the Bones

Criticism is never easy. I don't like criticism, but I have learned not to take it personally. Often our aversion to criticism comes from childhood. I know that I was criticized by family and peers, and I unfortunately made the mistake of criticizing my sons more than I should have. I have resolved to stop that pathology.

Nevertheless, constructive criticism is good. It aims to build people up and improve them. My former pastor, Craig Giles used to often say, "Eat the meat, spit out the bones!" I interpreted that to mean to take the things that you can benefit from and throw the rest out. You may be thinking, "What in the world does that have to do with self-confidence?" I would say, "A lot!"

You see, criticism is a big killer of self-esteem because it cuts at your self-worth. You must learn to jettison unhealthy criticism and embrace positive criticism. The unhealthy criticism seeks to tear you down. You must shun this feedback. Unfortunately, mean people will do or say things to intentionally harm others. You must realize that it is not about you but rather their own brokenness. Please don't take it personally. I pray people who are broken and mean spirited that they are healed, and I have empathy for them.

If you are fortunate, you will receive constructive criticism that aims to make you better. I consider that positive feedback. When you encounter mean spirited people, you may be able to leverage parts of their criticism as a personal growth opportunity. If part of it is true even if said in the wrong spirit, you can work to improve in that area of your life. In order maintain or grow your confidence, you should learn how to handle criticism and not let it diminish your value. Learn to eat the meat and spit out those bones!

Don't Be Afraid to Fail

A big part of being more confident is not being afraid to fail (I cover this in the chapter 18 "Face Your Fears"). I know there have been times when I did not do things because I was thinking "What if this fails or is not good enough." I remember a few years ago my cousin Tawanda suggested that I start doing videos. I said: "Yes, I want to do them but am not good at making them." Although I am not camera shy, I hesitated at first – I doubted my ability to do it, because I could not make a perfect video. However, I decided not to doubt and move forward with producing my own videos. They may not have been perfect, but I got started and gained more confidence in my ability to speak on camera. I believe that the videos inspired a few people along the way.

Don't let doubt or fear stop you from doing anything. If you fail, so what? Failure is not usually fatal. You can just keep trying. You must believe that you can do most things if you work hard and get the right experience. Don't let doubt impact your confidence or ability to do what is important!

Catch People Doing Right

It's not just about your becoming more confident, it is about helping others to be more confident as well. If you want to be more confident, you should not only elicit confidence for yourself but also for others. I believe an effective way to help others to be more confident is to catch them doing things right. It is easy to criticize people, but you are more impactful when you catch people doing well.

I remember listening to a soccer coach talk about how he helped others to be more confident by catching them doing something right. He used it to reinforce positive behaviors. This approach can help us as parents, leaders, spouses, etc. As you continue to work on your confidence, be intentional about building up others as well!

FOR REFLECTION
"Doubt kills more dreams than failure ever will."
~Suzy Kassem

- How would you rate your self-confidence on a scale of 1 to 10?
- Ask a few people who know you well how they rate your confidence to see if there are gaps between your perception of your confidence and theirs.
- What are barriers to your confidence?
- If you rated yourself at less than 9, what can you do to level up?
- What are you willing to do to elicit more confidence in others?

21 – UNDERSTAND YOUR VALUE AND FIT
Put Your Value Where It Belongs

I became the executive director of the HCEF on September 6, 2016. This experience was truly the manifestation of a dream job, where I operated at the center of my passion and purpose. However, the processes of walking in your passion and purpose and discovering your value are never easy. Just like the silversmith puts raw materials in the fire to burn off impurities and reveal shining precious metal, I go through continuous improvement processes.

I faced many challenges trying to establish myself as the new leader of the organization. It is never easy transitioning an organization from founder-led to one that is positioned for future growth and expansion. Founders work hard to create organizations and it is difficult for people to separate these individuals from the organization and acknowledge a new leadership with different direction.

It was incredibly challenging at times, and I was ready to resign! If what they say about things that do not kill you make you stronger is true, I should be Hercules about now! I can remember days when I struggled getting out of bed because I simply did not want to deal with the drama and challenges before me. I kept reminding myself that these experiences would make me better and that I would be able to use them to help others in the future. I resolved to focus not just on what I was doing, but why I was doing it.

I also faced staffing and fundraising challenges. Through the grace of God, much prayer and the support of friends, family, mentors, and other community leaders, I persevered. I left HCEF in a good place, doing important work to empower young people to break the cycle of homelessness through education. I miss my amazing team of people, who are compassionate, bright, highly engaged, innovative changemakers and a board that supported my leadership and vision for that great organization.

During the time I was wrapping up my website. I had been working on it for about six months with a young talent and new friend named Michael Anderson. We me that same year at a Pittsburgh Business Exchange (PBX) in June. Mike is a little shy but very confident. He has a smile that can melt snow and is ambitious, loyal, and passionate. He is younger than me but saw the potential of my vision and pushed, encouraged, and supported me to get my website up and running. I am grateful for him.

I wrote my first blog post in November 2017, and it was one of the first times that I was really putting myself out there in a very vulnerable and transparent way. The title of the post was: "*It Cut*

Like a Knife: Understanding Your Value and Where It Fits!" I chose that title because when my boss told me that I was not adding value, it literally cut like a knife and contributed to the emotional spiral and eventually, a job loss that was devastating for me. Here is an excerpt from the post:

> I remember it like it was yesterday. I was meeting with my manager, and he said, 'You are not adding value.' Wow. That really hurt! Although his words may have seemed cruel – and yes, I was devastated – he was right.
>
> I have always been an overachiever (didn't always realize it), but the fact that I was not adding value really cut like a knife. Although my manager may not have meant to degrade me, he did. In my mind, I heard subconsciously that I was worthless! To make a long story short, that job did not work out for me. I eventually moved on, which in the end, was in my best interest and the company's.
>
> Months down the road, I met with a counselor and shared the experience with him. He made a very poignant point: "Just because you don't add value in this job, does not mean that you won't add value somewhere else." Wow, his observation was a

eureka moment for me. My true watershed moment came after I owned and internalized that advice. It took me a little longer to get to that point. This brings me to my big lesson from this negative experience: Know your value and where it fits.

As I reflect on my interview experience for that job, I knew subconsciously that I should not have taken that position. I believe that I accepted it because I had a family to feed and not many other options. I quieted my internal voice. Following the experience and talking to friends and family, they said they did not think the job was a good fit for me. (Oh, now they tell me!)

These experiences helped me to reflect upon my value and where I fit in. I took the time to reevaluate my passion, purpose, and value. And yes, my counselor was right; I could and would add value in other places. This experience has well-positioned me to help others discover their value and purpose!

Shortly after this experience, I started doing consulting for a nonprofit organization, and the employees really appreciated my skill set and value. During this consulting role, I was further encouraged to pursue my professional dreams and continue my motivational speaking and inspiration. They encouraged me to share my message of hope, empowerment, and encouragement with all people. I met some of the most incredible people on Earth! Wow, it's awesome when people see your value! It is even more amazing when you discover and realize your own value and where it fits! Were it not for them or my negative experience, I would not have started www.seeds2fruitmotivation, nor would I have written this post today!

My newfound success and appreciation reinforced the words of that counselor who told me that others would appreciate my value. I was able to leverage my talents and passion, and yes, my value."

I shared this blog excerpt to help you realize the importance of not only understanding your value, but also leveraging it in the right place. In my case, I had value, but it was unrecognized and unappreciated in my old job. I hope that you can learn from my mistakes and truly learn and appreciate your own value so you can deploy it accordingly. After writing that post, I felt empowered. I was proud of myself for having the courage to put myself out there. My courage kickstarted my journey to discovering my value, passion, and purpose. It propelled me to write this book. Further, I better understood my value, passion purpose as I navigated the many leadership challenges at HCEF. Both experiences have given me greater clarity as to who I am and the value that I can add in the right space.

After reading this chapter, I hope you will be better equipped to assess, leverage, and grow your value in the right place!

Understand Your Value

Understand your talents and know your strengths and weaknesses. This has nothing to do with being vain or conceited but rather making sure that you are not discounting the value that you bring to the table. As part of understanding your value, it is critical that you assess where you are strongest and weakest. This level of awareness is empowering! It allows you to see areas you can leverage to propel you forward as well as areas where you may need to leverage others to help you improve or succeed.

One of my strengths is communication, but it is not editing or proofreading. And, therefore, when I wrote the initial blog post I reached out to my cousin Tawanda W. Johnson to do the edits. Her help prevented me from making a fool out of myself. Today, I leverage my wife, Marcia, to edit my blog. Assessing and understanding strengths and weaknesses is a good way to make sure that you are getting the most out of your value!

Know Where Your Value Fits In

Just because you have talents and skills, does not mean they fit in everywhere. Make sure you apply your talents where they will fit best. In my case, in my last banking role, I had certain skills and talents but did not take them to the right place. This created many problems for me. Although the experiences were very painful, I do not regret them, because they helped shape and mold me into the person I am today. If you can avoid certain headaches and traumas by taking your value to the right place, I highly recommend that you do this. Although I had many initial challenges in my leadership role at HCEF, my talents were being leveraged in the right place, in I way that I never could have done at the bank. Most importantly, I started a new leg of my career operating in my passion and purpose.

Your Value Is Not Defined by Your Job or Job Performance

Your value is your value, and it is intrinsic. It's not based on job performance or others' opinions. Too often people are in jobs that don't work out, because they are not a good fit. When looking for your next job, make sure that the culture and management appreciate your skills and recognize your value. Be mindful that if you don't get a promotion or get the recognition that you think you deserve, it does not define your value. God has placed the value in you, and no one can take that away. There is someone waiting for your unique talents and gifts! Your value is always the answer to a problem!

FOR REFLECTION
"Most hear the small voice telling them what they ought to be doing. Few have the courage to listen and act."
~Kerry Stith

- Are you confident about the value you bring to the table?
- What is your value? Do you feel like your value is appreciated in your current role?
- If not, what can you do to increase your value and apply it in the right space/place? If yes, what does your current employer do to make you feel valued?

22 – KEEP IT REAL
Learn to be Your Authentic Self

It takes courage to show up as your authentic self! In October 2019, I was invited to speak at a conference at Duquesne University. I debated what to wear in my mind. I could have worn a traditional suit or my "entrepreneur look" consisting of a nice blazer, casual shirt, and jeans. I decided to be myself and rock the "entrepreneur look." About four months later, I was speaking at another event, and a lady came up to me and said, "Thank you for wearing your jeans!" She went on to explain that her boss changed the dress code for their entire organization to allow jeans after seeing me speaking in mine. That blew my mind.

> **"It takes courage to show up as your authentic self!"**

The morning I wrestled trying to decide what to wear, I had no idea my decision to be my most authentic self would impact a whole organization. I was simply trying to wear something that was comfortable for me and at the same time respect the event protocol (there was no dress code specified). This little story exemplifies how deciding to show up authentically can inspire and affect others. I do realize that sometimes you must follow protocols. No matter what, having the courage to be your authentic self can do wonders for yourself and others! There is a lot of pressure to be like everyone else or to fit in.

Although I was usually encouraged to be myself growing up, there were still times when I let the fear of what others might think stop me from being my authentic self. As I became older and more confident, I decided to not let what others think about me dictate who I decide to be.

Even though I preach this message, I am challenged to live it. I created YouTube video called "I Still Believe." I wanted to give people hope for a brighter future during COVID-19 and to support the Black community during the various senseless killings of young Black men and women. I had the idea to start off singing "When You Believe," a song written for the 1998 DreamWorks film *The Prince of Egypt*. Although I believe I can sing, I was thinking that others may think it is silly and that I should not do it. Then I pushed against the voices of fear, humiliation and rejection and said to myself, "This is who I am and if people don't like it, that is fine, but I will push past my fears and be myself, no matter what!" The video did not have a lot of exposure on YouTube, but it had significantly more views on my other platforms compared to my other videos. Do you know why? I had the courage to show up authentically!

It takes courage to be your authentic self, especially given that others may not always value, appreciate, or understand you. Make sure that your version of keeping it real does not include being rude and mean to others. That is never acceptable.

Being your authentic self is challenging as you may face rejection or backlash. However, if you aren't living authentically, you are simply an imposter. Your body becomes a prison that incarcerates the real you who is trying to come out! My equation for keeping it real and being authentic is:

> *Keeping It Real = Living boldly and unapologetically who you are.*

I really try to be who I am as much as I can, from work to church to home and the community. I am sure my wife would prefer that I hold back as she is occasionally embarrassed. Still, she does show grace to allow me to be my authentic self, even though I can be a little crazy at times! No matter what, know that God created you and shaped you to be who you are. When you settle for what others have tried to make you to be, you are not keeping it real or living as your authentic self. A wise man once said, "Many people are born originals, but die as copies." Please don't go out like that… you deserve better. What does it take to keep it real or live authentically? I am glad you asked.

Know That You Are Enough

Getting to the place where you can live authentically is not easy, but it is worth the effort. I believe that you must come to the realization that who you are is enough. It does not matter how your parents treated you or how others made you feel. People have their own shortcomings, prejudices, and biases, but we cannot let that diminish who you are. Never be afraid to be who you are. You are enough. End of story! When you have the epiphany that you are enough, you will live like you are enough and will be your authentic self!

Know That Your Voice Matters

When you don't live openly and authentically, you diminish who you are. You are depriving the world of your voice. Who you are and what you say matters. You were uniquely created and there is no one like you. How you live and express yourself in all you do matters. God does not make mistakes. When he made you, he made someone special!

Take the time to see and explore the greatness that he has put in you. Start setting aside quiet time to listen to your voice. Make the time to understand what your inner voice is trying to tell you and how you can express it. As you get in touch with your voice and the value of that voice, you will not dare do anything to mute or diminish it. You need to own and acknowledge that your voice matters. Be courageous and don't let your fears stop you from being fully who you are. Why? When your authentic voice is muted, the world is incomplete.

Appreciate What Makes You Different

Earlier I talked about being dope and the power of diversity. It is important that you embrace what makes you different and special, because this will enable you to live authentically and keep it real! I once told my wife that I was a closeted nerd and she responded, "You are not in the closet!" Her response made me laugh and reminded me that everything about who we are makes us special. I have learned to embrace my nerdiness, coolness, craziness, and all that God has created me to be.

Reflect on themes covered in the previous chapter that speak to valuing differences and accepting yourself. When God made you, the mold was shattered. Why? Because what you have and who you are is so special. Don't deprive the universe and others of your awesomeness! Your difference is dope!

Speak And Live Your Truth

Never be afraid to share your story. I shared deeply personal things in this book. I used to be ashamed of my struggles, and this shame kept me in bondage. My good friend and motivational speaker Kierre Hawkins (aka Dream & Motivate) would say, "The struggle made me!"

Guess what? The struggle made you as well! Be proud of who you are and everything that has shaped and empowered you. Not only does speaking and living these truths empower you, but it empowers others. When you cannot speak, live, and walk in yourself truly, you are not living authentically. I'm not saying that you must share everything with everyone, but the courage to live and speak your truth will set you free and encourage others to pursue freedom. Don't be afraid to be who you are, even if others don't value or appreciate your authenticity.

FOR REFLECTION
"Be proud of who you are and everything that has shaped and empowered you."
~Carlos T. Carter

- Do you keep it real?
- What holds you back from living authentically?
- What will it take for you to overcome the barriers holding you back? Create a plan to overcome them.

23 – WHO YOU ARE WHEN NO ONE IS LOOKING
Integrity is the Lynchpin of Greatness

Integrity has a lot of definitions to different people. Dictionary.com defines integrity as "adherence to moral and ethical principles, soundness of moral character, honesty." I developed my definition after I read a book by Bill Hybles, retired pastor of Willow Creek, one of the largest churches in North America. Integrity is who you are when no one is looking.

Integrity is a word that is often used but not put into practice. It is difficult to be a person of integrity. There are situations and circumstances that tempt you to waiver. There is pressure to tell white lies to make yourself look better. You may be tempted to steal items from work when you know it is not appropriate. You may lie on a resume to get a job that you don't qualify for. The list goes on.

As leaders, it is critical that you do everything with integrity. At the end of the day, your name and reputation are all you have. One of my favorite proverbs says "A good name is more desirable than riches; to be esteemed is better than silver or gold. (Proverbs 22:1, NIV).

I mentioned this proverb to my middle son as he was asked to work at Ambridge Area High School while on school break. If he were a terrible worker and did not show integrity, I am certain that he would not have been called back each summer. I mentioned to him that he had a good name at the school, and it has created opportunities for him. Having integrity creates opportunities and opens doors. It is important to have character and to be a trustworthy person.

Integrity is critical for leadership, whether you have a formal leadership title or can influence others. I enjoy being a leader and a student of leadership. I enjoy coaching and inspiring other leaders to level up. There are several principles of leadership to which I ascribe, but the most important is "modeling the way" as discussed in Chapter 3.

As a leader, it is important to maintain a good name and character. It blows my mind that people can vote for and support leaders who do not have integrity. They may choose them as they like a few of their policies or rhetoric, but shouldn't integrity count for something?

As a leader and a leadership coach my integrity is all I have. It baffles my mind that people have excused leaders who perpetually lie. Integrity should transcend political affiliations because it is core to being a decent human being. No one is perfect, but if you cannot trust your leader to tell the truth that is a major issue. My team would not respect or follow my leadership if they could not trust me to tell the truth. I believe that integrity is a requirement of leaders, regardless of political affiliation.

It is easy to establish a beautifully written corporate or organizational value statement, but if leaders don't set the example, they are just empty words not worthy of the paper they are printed on. Although being a leader is incredibly challenging, setting a good example is critical to maintain your integrity.

There are people who express shock and horror when they hear about unethical or bad behavior rampant in organizations. You only need to look at the head to see why the tail is out of order. If you want your team to respect your leadership and live the mission and values of your organization, you must model the way. One of my favorite leadership gurus John C. Maxwell, says: "Followers may doubt what leaders say, but usually believe what they do!" No leader is perfect, but leaders will never teach until they practice what they preach!

As you walk through life, make sure that you live it and walk it with integrity. We don't need more perfect leaders; we need people who are committed to setting good examples for others to follow. Many subscribe to the Machiavellian approach of doing whatever it takes to get results. I believe that it is critical to live and lead with integrity.

What Type of Legacy Do You Want to Leave?

A good way to maintain your integrity is to reflect on how you want to be remembered. Do not obsess over what others think about you. Be mindful of the legacy you want to leave for your family and community. Especially if you have children, what legacy do you want to pass down to them.

I want to be known as a man of integrity who left people and places better than I found them. I want to be remembered as a man who empowered people to discover their value, passion, and purpose, and the greatness that is within. I want my children to look at my life as a positive example to model. I encourage you to reflect on the legacy you want to leave and start living it out today. A wise person once said, "Your true legacy is not just reflected in your children, but in how your grandchildren turn out." Live a life that reflects integrity as it will have an impact on generations to come. John C. Maxwell said: "Someday, people will summarize your life in a single sentence. My advice is to pick it now!" To this, I will add: "Live it now!"

Model the Way

I don't want to beat this into the ground, but you must set an example. People should be able to look at your actions and see that they are aligned with your words. If you want to see what a person is really thinking and believing, pay more attention to their actions than their words. Their actions tell you what they really believe. One of my favorite quotes by rapper Missy Elliot is, "Don't talk about it, be about it!"

What Does Your Integrity or Lack of Integrity Say About You?

Integrity is living a life where your actions are in line with your words; it is doing what you say you are going to do and striving to maintain the highest standards of honesty, even when it isn't convenient. Don't let anything tarnish your reputation. When you make mistakes, don't be afraid to admit them. It takes years to build integrity, but it can be lost through one bad decision!

Evaluate Who You Are When No One Is Looking

The true test of integrity is who you are when no one is looking. If you could lie, cheat, and steal in secret, will you do it? I would proffer that your integrity should be the same in the light as the dark. After all, what is done in the dark will come to light. Continue to evaluate your decisions and integrity to make sure that it is the same at all times. Strive to leave a legacy of integrity and honor that your children and grandchildren can follow. Who you are when no one is looking is the ultimate measure of your integrity and greatness.

FOR REFLECTION
"We don't need more perfect leaders; we need people who are committed to setting good examples for others to follow."
~Carlos T. Carter

- Have you lived a life of integrity? If not, what can you do to get on the right path?
- Remember what John C. Maxwell said about someone summarizing your life in a single sentence. What is the sentence you want people to write about your life?
- What can you do to maintain integrity when no one is looking?

GET ON THE ROAD TO GREATNESS

Now what? You have just read a book that has given you insight and inspiration, but you cannot keep living the same way. Are you willing to push yourself to aim higher?

Change starts with your thoughts; it starts with wanting to commit to doing things differently. If you want to achieve your desired goals, you must have a plan. It requires a strong faith, knowing that anything is possible when you believe. You must resolve to do what it takes to become the best version of yourself and to discover and realize the greatness that is within you! It requires that you believe in yourself and the greatness that has been imbued in you!

Passion, purpose, and service to others are the cornerstones of greatness. You were created for something bigger than yourself. Position yourself to lead with passion and purpose and achieve the energy and drive to strive, to give, and live a life that not only empowers yourself, but others. True and pure greatness is defined well by this Martin Luther King, Jr. quote: "Everybody can be great, because anybody can serve. You don't have to have a college degree to serve. You don't have to make your subject and verb agree to serve. You only need a heart full of grace. A soul generated by love."

On your road to greatness, you will have to face your fears. Get out of your comfort zone and have the courage to tell that voice that says that you cannot do something to "shut up." Be your authentic self and live a life of integrity even when you are challenged to take shortcuts or compromise your values. Learn when to say "yes" to things that propel you forward and no to what holds you back.

You must understand your value and that your difference is dope, even when others reject you because you don't look or think like them. You must know that you were created for a purpose and that God does not make people by accident. If you are alive, there is purpose to your life. The person you are and what you bring to the table may be the answer to someone else's problem.

Continue to dream; there are no limits to your potential. No matter your race, age, gender, zip code, or sexual orientation, you are special and created for greatness. Be willing to courageously face the big stuff, because you were created for purpose and greatness. You cannot let anything stop you from getting there even if you are not where you want to be or are trying to take things to the next level. Always remain hopeful and keep a positive attitude. Never become so stuck mind that you don't believe in change. Change is always possible; if you have breath in your lungs, you can change. It is easy to become negative and discouraged, but I urge you to fight it as if your life depends on it. Believing that *the best is yet to come* is the fuel for change and paves the road to greatness!

It's going to take hard work, grit, sweat, and tears. Reflect and push yourself even when you don't feel like it. Never give up on your dreams, never give up on you. Keep leading and serving with passion and purpose. Your willingness to read this book and do the reflection exercises is evidence that you are hungry to become the best version of yourself and discover and unlock the greatness that is within you!

You can do it my friend . . . you got this!

"Your dreams and goals may seem out of reach, but you can achieve them if you work hard, push, and believe."

~Carlos T. Carter

ABOUT THE AUTHOR

Carlos faced many challenges in life: poverty, fatherlessness, depression, and job losses. Despite those obstacles, he remained steadfast in his desire to succeed. He became the first in his family to attend college and rose to the level of senior vice president at Bank of America.

Carlos is a freelance writer and has several published articles. He is a gifted singer and often incorporates singing into his motivational presentations. As an actor, he has starred in several plays and commercials, and was an extra in the last movie with the late great Chadwick Boseman: Ma Rainey's Black Bottom. A recognized leader, Carlos is the former Executive Director of Homeless Children's Education Fund (HCEF) where he empowered youth to break the cycle of homelessness through education.

Today, Carlos is President and CEO of the Urban League of Greater Pittsburgh, where he works to empower African Americans and other marginalized communities to achieve economic self-reliance, parity, power, and civil rights. He is the father of three sons: Elijah, Daylon, and Isaiah, and has been married to his beautiful wife, Marcia, for over twenty years.

Carlos T. Carter is committed to inspiring and empowering others to discover their greatness by leading with passion and purpose as a motivational speaker, leadership coach, and blogger.

Visit www.seeds2fruitmotivation.com to book Carlos for your next event or to subscribe for inspirational updates.

Follow Carlos on social media:
@seeds2fruitmotivation or Carlos T. Carter

REFERENCES

Carnegie, Dale. (1984) "How to Stop Worrying and Start Living"

Ekman, Paul. "What Causes Fear?"

Jones, K. and Okun, T. (2001) "White" Organizational Culture From Dismantling Racism: A Workbook for Social Change Groups

Maxwell, John C. Maxwell (1998 and 2007) "The 21 Irrefutable Laws of Leadership."

Pink, Daniel H. "Drive : The Surprising Truth About What Motivates Us", (2019)

Lesco, Levi. (2018) "I Declare War" p. 249

Sanders, Oswald, J. (2007) *Spiritual Leadership* p. 155

Lexico.com definitions of "Networking"

Peal, Norman, V. (1952) *The Power of Positive Thinking.* pps., 94, 98